RA

## BOOK 2

Junior Cycle SPHE

# MY life

## Stephanie Mangan

FOLENS
Wellbeing

## FREE eBook
## on purchase of this textbook*

Simply...

**1** Scratch the foil below to reveal your unique licence code.

**2** Visit **folensonline.ie/redeem**

**3** Follow the simple steps outlined there.

DSBT-UDMK

*Teachers – please go to FolensOnline.ie

## FOLENS

First published in 2017 by Folens Publishers

Hibernian Industrial Estate, Greenhills Road, Tallaght, Dublin 24

© Stephanie Mangan 2017

**Illustrations:** EMC Design

ISBN 978-1-78090-754-3

## Acknowledgements

The authors and publisher would like to thank the following for permission to use copyright material: iStock and Shutterstock.

The publisher has made every effort to contact all copyright holders but if any have been overlooked, we will be pleased to make any necessary arrangements.

Any links or references to external websites should not be construed as an endorsement by Folens of the content or views of these websites.

# Contents

going to Collage

# Preface

Welcome to Second Year. I hope that you are now settled in to secondary school. I also hope that you enjoyed SPHE last year, especially the variety of activities such as group work, walking debates, pair work, online research and class discussions. This year there will be plenty more of these activities as you learn about:

* Applying decision-making skills in a variety of situations

* Personal and social skills to address pressure to smoke, to drink alcohol and/or to use other substances

* Developing a sense of belonging in school, at home and in the wider community

* Improving your communication skills in support of responsible, informed decision-making about relationships and sexual health

* What it means to live with mental ill-health and a variety of coping skills and strategies to build your resilience

There is no exam in SPHE, but your teacher will tell you if you will be doing a classroom-based assessment and will tell you more about how SPHE is assessed in your school.

Like last year, you are encouraged to discuss SPHE at home with your parents/ guardians or family, especially sensitive topics that may upset or concern you. Remember, too, that having a personal learning journal at home is a great way to reflect on your learning and manage your thoughts.

I wish you a great school year and sincerely hope that you enjoy the learning experience of SPHE with *My Life 2.*

*Stephanie Mangan*

Stephanie Mangan

# Introduction

There are lots of activities in this book that may involve working together or working on your own. There might not always be time to do every activity, so your teacher will decide which activities your class will do. Below are the activity symbols that you will see in the book with an explanation of what each symbol means.

### Wellbeing indicators

The Wellbeing indicators are Active, Responsible, Connected, Resilient, Respected and Aware. You will see these symbols at the beginning of each lesson to denote which Wellbeing indicators are developed in that lesson.

### Learning outcomes

Learning outcomes are stated at the beginning of each strand to give you a clear indication of what you are expected to learn in that strand.

### Learning intentions

Learning intentions are clearly visible at the beginning of each lesson. They state what you should know, understand or be able to do by the end of that lesson.

### Key words

You will notice key words at the beginning of each lesson and definitions in key word boxes throughout the book.

### Warm-up activities

Each lesson starts with an optional warm-up activity.

### Individual work

When you see this symbol, you have to do the work on your own.

### Pair work

This means that you work together as a pair. Your teacher will assign you a partner.

### Group work

This symbol indicates that this activity should be done in groups. Your teacher will divide you into groups.

### Class discussion

This means that the class should discuss a particular topic. Your teacher will lead the discussion.

### Class activity

This means that the class should work together. Your teacher will give roles or jobs to individuals or groups.

### Numeracy

This symbol means that you will have an opportunity to use and improve your numeracy skills.

### Lesson link

You will see the lesson link symbol where a topic links with another lesson in *My Life*.

### Subject link

You will see this symbol when a topic relates to another Junior Cycle subject.

### Go online

This symbol indicates that you should find further information on the internet at home or at school with your teacher's or parent's permission.

### FolensOnline 'play'

There are many digital resources for *My Life* on FolensOnline. These include:

* Animations
* Videos
* PowerPoint presentations
* Links to other websites

Activities in this book are often based on these digital resources.

### Positive message

You will see a positive message exercise at the end of every lesson. This activity helps to improve your problem-solving and coping skills by using information that you learned in that lesson.

### Rapid recap

At the end of each lesson, the rapid recap encourages you to revise what you have learned and to focus on what you need to find out. You can show this to your parents to let them know what you are learning about in SPHE.

### Assessment idea

Your teacher will tell you whether you are to do this assessment. He/she will give you guidelines, assign groups and give a submission date.

### Homework

This is the homework for you to complete at home relating to each lesson.

### Personal learning journal

Your personal learning journal is a private record that you keep at home. You are encouraged to write in it throughout the year to reflect on what you have learned in SPHE.

### Strand review

SPHE offers opportunities to support all eight key skills of the Junior Cycle curriculum. A strand review section appears at the end of each strand and is based on these key skills. This can help you to reflect on what you have learned, identify strengths and select areas for improvement.

# Who am I?

This strand focuses on developing self-awareness and building self-esteem.

## Strand learning outcomes

- Identify short-, medium- and long-term personal goals and ways in which they might be achieved

- Apply decision-making skills in a variety of situations

- Source appropriate and reliable information about health and wellbeing

- Participate in informed discussions about the impact of physical, emotional, psychological and social development in adolescence

- Appreciate the importance of respectful and inclusive behaviour in promoting a safe environment free from bias and discrimination

# 1. I am me

At the end of this lesson, you will:

 Have reflected on your experience of First Year

 Have examined what it means to be mature

 Have thought about the year ahead

 **Maturity**

**Aware**
**Resilient**
**Responsible**

Find someone in your class who fits the criteria below. They must sign their name in the space provided. You can't use the same person twice. See who can finish first.

| This summer I ... | Signature |
|---|---|
| Went to Spain | Ignacio |
| Went to the Gaeltacht | — |
| Swam in the sea | Aliza - vanessa - william - Adam |
| Went to a concert | Rachel |
| Rode a horse | Wenyi |
| Got sunburnt | Abigal    iris   vaneesa |
| Had a part-time job | Aiza |
| Saw a famous person | Ana Winsten  william. |
| Got my hair cut | Sophia |

# Maturity

You have probably matured a lot since you finished primary school, maybe without you even realising it. You are on the path to becoming a fully developed mature adult. However, teenagers often disagree or argue with adults because the teenager thinks that they are already fully mature and an adult disagrees.

Eventually you will be a mature person capable of making your own wise and responsible decisions, but this takes time. Some people could be very mature at age 16, while some are still immature at age 36!

**Maturity** is the full development of someone or something.

Read the list below, which describes some characteristics of a mature person. Discuss what each statement means.

A mature individual:

- Takes responsibility for their mistakes
- Doesn't need someone to remind them to brush their teeth or other basic means of personal care
- Is able to control and deal with emotions
- Makes wise choices and thinks about what would benefit them most in the future
- Puts other people before themselves
- Can make and stick to plans
- Considers the feelings of others
- Knows their strengths and weaknesses
- Is confident in their abilities
- Is responsible with their belongings
- Can deal with constructive criticism

1. Read back over the list on the previous page and ask yourself: 'Is this true for me?' Use the list to help you think of two ways you can try to become more mature and write them below, e.g. 'Makes wise choices – I could eat less junk food so that I am healthier'.

_____

_____

2. Write about a time when you think that you acted very maturely. (You don't have to share your answer with the class.)

_____

_____

_____

## Looking back

Now that you are in Second Year you hopefully have fewer concerns or worries about school and feel more of a part of the school community. Think back to this time last year. What were you worried about? Are you worried about the same things this year?

Think about your experience of First Year, then answer the following questions.

1. What was the best thing about First Year?

_You made new friends_

2. What was the worst thing about First Year?

_Getting look down | picked on by 6th year_

3. Who supported you or helped you with a problem in First Year?

_House person_

4. What are you most proud of from last year?

_Scifest_

5. List some of the emotions you felt when you were starting First Year.

_scared, nervous_

In groups, think about the First Years starting school this week. What three pieces of advice would you give them?

_Don't be scared and don't worry_
_Get involved_
_Do your best_

Imagine that your school has organised a foreign exchange visit for you during Second Year. In your copy, write your first email to the boy or girl who will be visiting you in January, and who you will then visit in March. Introduce yourself – tell them about your personality, hobbies, likes and dislikes and mention some fun activities that you might do when they visit.

## Where to find help

1. Last year in SPHE you learned about websites that offer advice or that can help you with particular problems. Write an example of each website in the space below.

   Mental health: _____

   Puberty: _____

   Bullying: _____

2. Last year you also made a list of people in school who could help you if you need it. Some of these people are still the same, but some may have changed. Fill in the following table.

| | |
|---|---|
| **Year head** | Mr Malone + Mrs Cummins |
| **Class tutor** | Ms Geraatty |
| **Principal** | Mr Ronan |
| **Vice-principal** | Mr O'Brudair    Ms. Marshall |
| **Guidance counsellor** | Ms. McGinn   Ms. Tanner |
| **Chaplain or other person in school I can ask for help** | Reverend Campion |

# Looking forward

In pairs, make a list of the things you are looking forward to in Second Year. Share your answers with the class.

– Getting lunch early :)

– Art & Business

# Rules for SPHE class

Last year in SPHE you wrote and signed a contract that set the ground rules for your SPHE class. Can you remember the rules and the sanctions for breaking the rules? Rewrite this contract in your copy and make any changes that the class feels are necessary.

Write a positive message to a Second Year who has just moved to your school. He or she doesn't know anyone and is nervous about fitting in.

Everyone is very nice and kind.

Don't be nervous

# Rapid recap

**3**

Topics we discussed today:

1. _Maturity_
2. _1st year_
3. _2nd Year_

**2**

People or places I could find out more information on this lesson from:

1. _____
2. _____

**1**

Something in today's lesson that I would like to learn more about:

1. _____

**Parent's/guardian's signature** _____

(Your teacher will tell you if this should be signed each week.)

Check the school notice board, bulletin or website to find out about one event or activity that you can look forward to this term.

Complete your personal learning journal at home.

# 2. Looking after myself

**At the end of this lesson, you will:**

 Be aware of your responsibilities for your own safety and the safety of others

 Be aware of the causes of accidents in a variety of situations and the steps that can be taken to avoid them

Key word

abc Independent

🧠 **Aware**

🌱 **Resilient**

👤 **Responsible**

Find as many possible dangers as you can in the picture. When you have found 10 dangers, put your hand up.

## Becoming responsible for your safety

As you mature and become more independent, you are expected to make more responsible decisions that affect your wellbeing, including decisions that affect your personal safety. As a child, your parents or guardians were always responsible for your safety. Now that you are older and more independent, you must take more responsibility for your own personal safety. If you have younger siblings, you may be expected to share some of the responsibilities of looking after them too.

**Independent**
abc Capable of thinking and acting without consulting others.

Discuss the different responsibilities and independence you have as a teenager that you did not have as a child, e.g. going to the shop by yourself.

## Home safety check

The following list of questions has been designed to examine your awareness of and responsibility for your personal safety in the home. Answer yes or no to see how aware and responsible you are.

|   |   | Yes | No |
|---|---|---|---|
| 1. | When you are cooking, do you stay at the cooker? | ✓ | |
| 2. | Do you unplug all electrical appliances when they are not needed, including chargers? (Actually unplug them, not just turn off the switch!) | | ✓ |
| 3. | If you light candles, are they in a proper holder and never left unattended? | ✓ | |
| 4. | If you have fairy lights in your bedroom, are they unplugged every night? | ✓ | |
| 5. | If there are small children at home, do you always close the stair gate? | | |

| | | YES | NO |
|---|---|:---:|:---:|
| 6. | Is your bedroom floor area clear of clothes and other clutter in case you need to make an escape? | ✓ | |
| 7. | If your bedroom windows are locked, is the key in them in case you need to make an escape? | ✓ | |
| 8. | If you are the last one up at night, do you make sure that all doors are closed before going to bed? | ✓ | |
| 9. | Do you know where the keys are to get out of the house in the event of an emergency at night? | ✓ | |
| 10. | Do you know your parents' or guardians' mobile phone numbers? | ✓ | |
| 11. | Do you know what to do if the smoke alarm or carbon monoxide alarm sounds? | ✓ | |

If you answered 'no' to any of the questions, you should correct the problem as soon as possible.

# Safety on farms

Around 2,000 injuries occur on Irish farms each year and unfortunately there are many fatalities too. Many people who grow up on farms are very comfortable with their surroundings, but sometimes when people are too comfortable, their safety is at risk because they are not looking out for possible dangers. On the other hand, some people who have very little knowledge of farms may visit a farm at some stage and can be in danger if they don't know about things that could be dangerous.

Read the advice on FolensOnline on how to stay safe on a farm, whether you are a visitor or you live or work on a farm. If you know a lot about farms, you may be able to offer more advice.

# Safety in the city

Just like some students may be very familiar with farms, others may be very familiar with the city. Most people in cities are just nice, normal people going about their everyday lives. However, urban areas do tend to have higher than average crime rates, especially in inner-city areas. Therefore, it is always important to be aware of your own safety in the city.

In groups, draw up a list of safety tips designed for a tourist from another country who is spending a week in a city near you. Write the tips in your copy.

# ■ Be safe at night ■

You should always try to avoid walking alone at night, regardless of whether you are in a rural or built-up area, as it is much easier for a person to commit a crime in the dark. To avoid such a situation, always follow these guidelines.

* Have credit in your phone and have it charged. Know your parents' or guardians' number so that you can ring them from someone else's phone if necessary.

* Make clear arrangements beforehand about how you will get home from a particular place.

* Stay with your friends.

* Be aware of your surroundings and know where you are going.

If you find that you do have to walk alone at night, follow these tips to keep safe.

* Walk where there are streetlights.

* Wear something bright so that you can be seen by cars, particularly on country roads. If all your outer clothing is dark, you could tie something bright or white on your arm. It would be useful to keep a reflector belt or jacket in your bag for use in such situations.

* Stay on main roads or streets where there are other people, even if there is a shortcut.

* If you think that someone is following you, don't be embarrassed to call in to someone's house and ask for help or to use their phone.

* Never accept a lift from a stranger, even if they appear to be 'nice' or 'normal'.

* Don't be afraid or embarrassed to ask the Gardaí for help.

Does anyone in the class have any other tips that you may have learned from your parents or guardians or perhaps at a self-defence class? Has anyone in the class ever found themselves in such a situation? If so, how did they feel and what did they do?

Your class could invite a local Garda to talk to your class about personal safety for teenagers. Draw up a list of questions that you would ask him or her.

1. In groups, make a list of tips on how a young person can stay safe when they are home alone or babysitting. Share your advice with the class.

- Lock doors + windows
- Know emergency numbers
- If you have a baby install baby protective devices.

2. Make a list of places in your area that are thought to be unsafe.

- Forests
- The slip road
- Concerts
-

Write a positive message to a 15-year-old who gets anxious when at home alone.

# Rapid recap

**3**

Topics we discussed today: ~~Sta~~

1. ~~Stafty~~ Safty at home
2. " city
3. " farm

**2**

People or places I could find out more information on this lesson from:

1. _____

2. _____

**1**

Something in today's lesson that I would like to learn more about:

1. _____

**Parent's/guardian's signature** _____

(Your teacher will tell you if this should be signed each week.)

Go through the home safety check on pages 10–11 with your parent or guardian.
Discuss any points that you answered 'no' to and discuss any concerns.

Complete your personal learning journal at home.

# 3. Setting goals

**At the end of this lesson, you will:**

 Have set personal goals for this year

Have thought about who influences you

Key words
abc

Influence
Goal
Obstacle

 I can't do it

**Aware**
**Responsible**
**Connected**

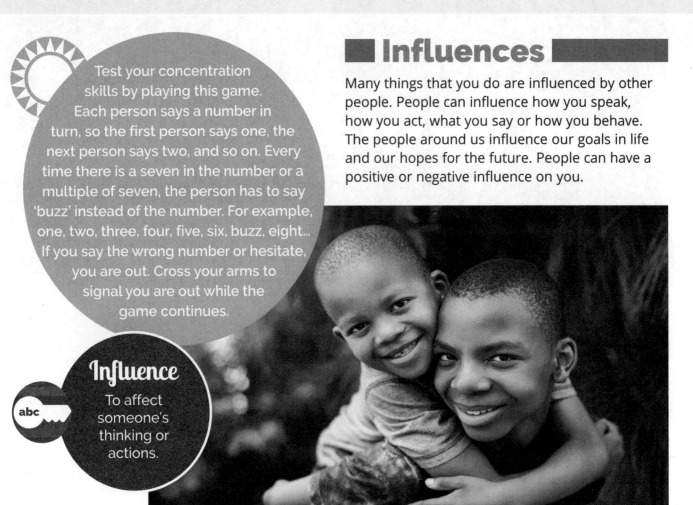

Test your concentration skills by playing this game. Each person says a number in turn, so the first person says one, the next person says two, and so on. Every time there is a seven in the number or a multiple of seven, the person has to say 'buzz' instead of the number. For example, one, two, three, four, five, six, buzz, eight... If you say the wrong number or hesitate, you are out. Cross your arms to signal you are out while the game continues.

# Influences

Many things that you do are influenced by other people. People can influence how you speak, how you act, what you say or how you behave. The people around us influence our goals in life and our hopes for the future. People can have a positive or negative influence on you.

## Influence

**abc** To affect someone's thinking or actions.

Think about how the things that you do are influenced by other people.

| Things I do | Who influences this? |
|---|---|
| The clothes I wear | time, friends, celebrities |
| The food I eat | mom, me |
| Things I say or how I speak | ~~grandparents~~ + family |
| My manners | family + Parents |
| How I behave in school | Myself + parents |
| My attitude to schoolwork | parents |
| My hopes for the future | school, myself |

# Goals

You may remember from First Year that goals should be:

✳ Within your power to make happen through your own actions

✳ Important to you personally

✳ Something you have a reasonable chance of achieving

Goals can be short, medium or long term.

✳ A short-term goal could be getting your homework done by Friday.

✳ A medium-term goal could be being able to run 5K in three months' time.

✳ A long-term goal could be practising piano for 30 minutes every day so that you pass your exam next year.

When you set goals, it helps you to focus and gives you a target to aim for. Occasionally people and things will get in the way of your goals and you will have to find a way to overcome this.

## Goal
A goal is something that you aim to achieve.

Can anyone share a long-term goal that they have in life, such as travelling the world, becoming an actress or being the first person in their family to get a college degree?

This exercise will help you to set a long-term goal for school this year. In your copy, you could also use this table to set some short- and medium-term goals for school too. Read the example first, then set your own long-term goal for your schoolwork.

| My goal | To get better than a C in all maths tests |
|---|---|
| To be achieved by | Christmas |
| Steps I must take | Always do my homework. Study for every test. Ask the teacher when I don't understand something. |
| What might get in the way and what can I do about this? | I could be distracted in class, so I will sit at the front. If it gets too hard, I will work harder at home and watch tutorial videos again at home. |
| Who can help me? | My brother My maths teacher |

ALIZA

ALIZA        ALIZA                    Hi

# ALIZA

Go to FolensOnline and watch Mark's story, in which he talks about his love for football and his dreams for the future, then answer the following questions.

**Obstacle**

Something that may prevent you from achieving your goal.

1. What is Mark's goal?

_____

_____

2. What obstacles does he have to overcome?

_____

_____

3. Did you ever overcome obstacles to achieve a goal?

_____

_____

## Being involved in my community

In First Year you learned the advantages of being part of your local community. These include: **CSPE**

* Making new friends
* Improving your mental health and mood
* Helping others
* Learning new skills and hobbies

Make a list of ways that you could become more active in your local community this year.

_____

_____

_____

_____

Using the above suggestions, decide on one medium-term goal that will help you to become more involved in your community this year.

_____

_____

# Exercise

In First Year you learned about the benefits of physical activity and exercise. Most research shows that physical activity declines during the teenage years, usually between 13 and 15 years of age. As a class, can you think of reasons for this? CP-PE

Being more active can:

* Strengthen your bones and muscles

* Help control your weight

* Reduce your risk of heart disease

* Improve your mental health and mood

* Increase your chances of living longer

* Reduce your risk of some cancers

 Write one short-term and one long-term goal in relation to your physical activity for this school year.

_____

_____

# Summary of my goals

| Goal | To be achieved by |
| --- | --- |
| | |
| | |
| | |
| | |
| | |

 Write a message to a First Year who didn't achieve her goal, which was to get an A in her Christmas exam.

_____

_____

_____

## ⏱ Rapid recap

**3** Topics we discussed today:

1. _____

2. _____

3. _____

**2** People or places I could find out more information on this lesson from:

1. _____

2. _____

**1** Something in today's lesson that I would like to learn more about:

1. _____

**Parent's/guardian's signature** _____

(Your teacher will tell you if this should be signed each week.)

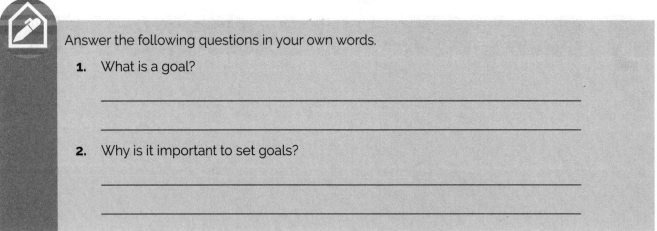

Answer the following questions in your own words.

1. What is a goal?

_____

_____

2. Why is it important to set goals?

_____

_____

Complete your personal learning journal at home.

# 4. Being focused

**At the end of this lesson, you will:**

Understand how motivation affects your achievement of goals

Practise study skills that will help you achieve your goals in relation to schoolwork

Key word
abc
**Motivation**

🧠 **Aware**
🏃 **Responsible**

Your teacher will put up an Agree sign and a Disagree sign in different corners of the classroom. Stand at the right place in the classroom according to whether you agree or disagree with the following statements. Remember to think for yourself – don't just follow the crowd.

- Money makes the world go round.
- Health is more important than wealth.
- I go to school because I want to learn.
- I would rather have a job that I love with poor pay than a job that I hate with brilliant pay.
- I don't care what other people think about me.
- I would love to be famous.
- Rich people are happier than poor people.
- Love makes the world go round.
- I only go to school because I have to.
- I work hard in school because I want to get into a college course that I like.
- People can be poor and happy.

# Motivation

To do well in life, it is important to understand motivation and know what motivates you. Everyone is motivated by different things. For example, one footballer might work hard and practise all the time because he wants the honour and glory of playing for his country. Another footballer might work hard because he wants money and fame. We all need motivation to help us do things that are hard.

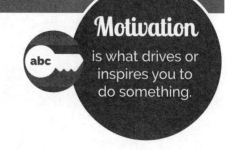

**Motivation** is what drives or inspires you to do something.

If you want to do well in school and get good exam results, there have to be things that motivate you. It is important that you do things for the right reasons. Read through the list below and rate the importance of each statement from 1 to 10, with 1 being the most important.

I want to get good results because...

| | |
|---|---|
| Then I can get into any college that I want. | ✓ |
| My parents will be proud of me. | ✓ |
| Everyone will see just how smart I am. | ✓ |
| I want to prove my parents/teachers wrong. | ✓ |
| Everyone else will be jealous. | ✓ |
| I deserve good results for working so hard. | ✓ |
| I can get a job that pays lots of money. | ✓ |
| It will prove that I am smarter than my brother/sister. | ✓ |
| I can get a job that I will love. | ✓ |
| I will be proud of myself. | ✓ |

# Study skills

Last week you set goals to improve your schoolwork. In order to achieve these goals, you must know how to study effectively. Everybody studies and learns differently because we all have different learning styles or ways of learning. Understanding your learning style will help you to study well.

Take the quiz on FolensOnline to find out more about your learning style. Many people use more than one learning style.

# Ways of learning and studying

Try the following ways of learning and studying to see if they suit your learning style.

## Mnemonics

This method is useful when you need to remember a list, particularly for auditory learners. You take the first letter of each word and make a sentence using those letters. For example, to remember the colours of the rainbow:

**R**ed, **O**range, **Y**ellow, **G**reen, **B**lue, **I**ndigo, **V**iolet

**R**ichard **O**f **Y**ork **G**ave **B**attle **I**n **V**ain

You could also take the first letter of each word in the list and use those letters to make one word. For example, the properties of water are that it is **c**olourless, **o**dourless and **t**asteless, so you could use the word **COT** to help you to remember.

In groups, use mnemonics to help you remember this list of nutrients:

Protein          Vitamins          Carbohydrates

Fats             Minerals

## Mind maps

A mind map is a diagram used to represent words, ideas, tasks or other items linked to and arranged around a central key word or idea. Mind maps can be used to generate or structure, organise and classify ideas. Visual and tactile learners may benefit more from making mind maps, while auditory learners may benefit more from making the mind map and then explaining it to someone or having it explained to them. See an example of a mind map on the next page.

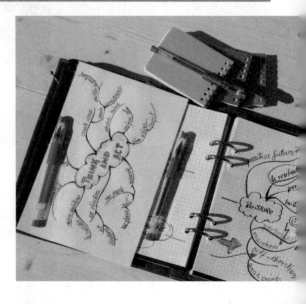

You won't have time to make a mind map now in class, but you can do it for homework to revise a topic you are studying during the week. Try to summarise a chapter or topic from one of your textbooks. You could also use a mind map to summarise the role and characteristics of all the characters in a play or book that you are studying.

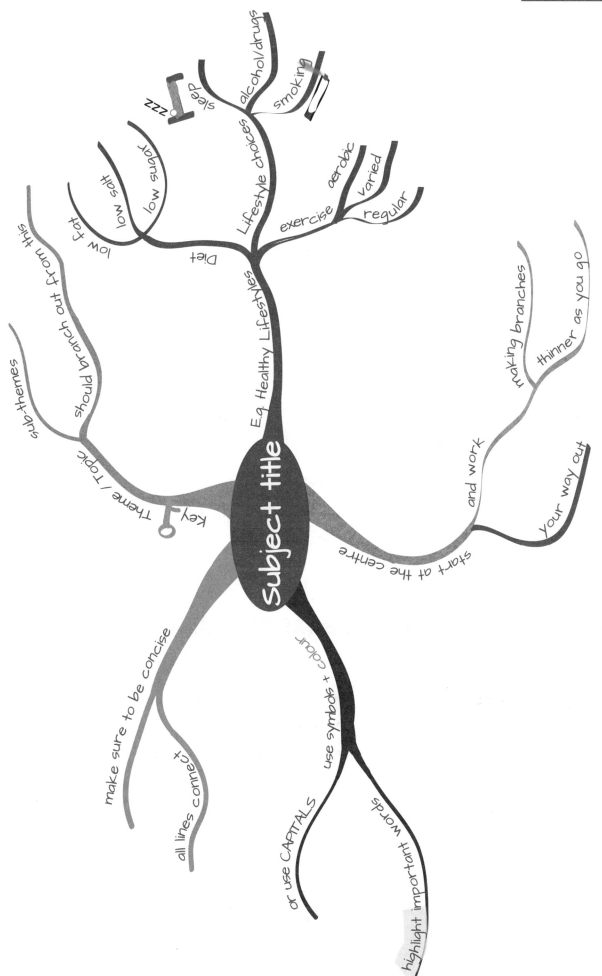

# Flash cards

Flash cards are a fast way to revise before a test or exam. Flash cards can suit all learning styles. They summarise the main points from a topic and can help you to organise what you need to learn. Write the topic on the front of your card and the main points that you need to remember on the back. Make them when you are studying and then use them to revise before a test. Below is a sample of a flash card.

# Taking notes

One method of studying that is particularly suited to visual and tactile learners is taking notes. If you start taking or making notes now, you can use them to study and revise for your summer tests and for your Junior Certificate. Try to make some notes every day on what you did in each subject. The purpose of notes is to sum up what you have learned so that you won't have to read the whole textbook again when you get to Third Year. Follow these guidelines for taking notes.

Write a heading.
- Use bullet points.
- Use short sentences.
- Use different colours.
- Underline the important points.
- Highlight the important words.
- Use symbols instead of long words. ☺
- Write the lesson/chapter and page number at the end for reference, e.g. Lesson 7, page 36.

In pairs, pick any page from any book in your bag and summarise it following the guidelines on the previous page.

_____

_____

_____

_____

_____

# Pamela's story

Go to FolensOnline and watch Pamela's story. In pairs, answer the following questions.

1.  Why did Pamela change her approach to study?

    _____

    _____

2.  Describe two changes Pamela made to her usual routine to incorporate study.

    _____

    _____

3.  Describe two methods Pamela used to study.

    _____

    _____

4.  Suggest two other methods that Pamela could use to help her study.

    _____

    _____

Write a positive message to a Second Year who enjoys speaking French in class but who struggles to learn his French vocabulary and spellings for homework.

_____

_____

_____

_____

# Rapid recap

### 3

Topics we discussed today:

1. _____

2. _____

3. _____

### 2

People or places I could find out more information on this lesson from:

1. _____

2. _____

### 1

Something in today's lesson that I would like to learn more about:

1. _____

**Parent's/guardian's signature** _____

(Your teacher will tell you if this should be signed each week.)

Make a sample flash card below to help you remember something you have to learn for homework tonight.

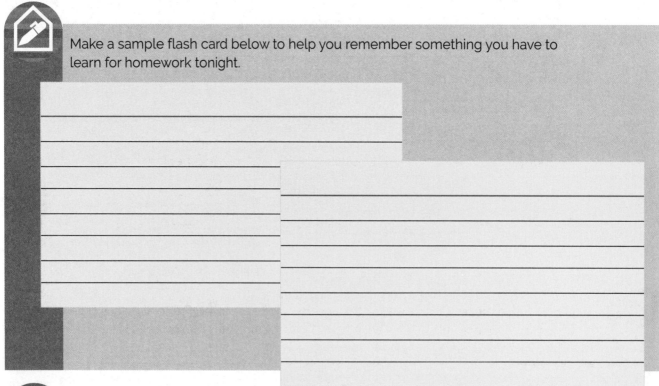

Complete your personal learning journal at home.

# 5. Staying well

**At the end of this lesson, you will:**

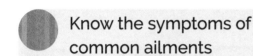 Know the symptoms of common ailments

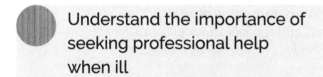 Understand the importance of seeking professional help when ill

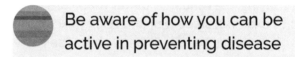 Be aware of how you can be active in preventing disease

Have thought about your own decisions in relation to disease prevention

 Key words
abc

*Ailment*
*Symptom*
*Fatal*
*Hereditary*

Resilient
Aware
Responsible

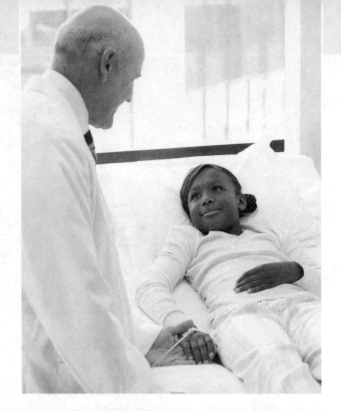

This lesson deals with illness and disease. Some students in the class may be affected by these issues or have family members who are affected by them, so please be sensitive when expressing your opinions.

Take a minute now to think of anyone you know who is suffering or has suffered from disease. Think about a happy time that you shared with them.

# Illness

The old saying 'prevention is better than cure' is very true. It is important that we eat healthily, exercise, sleep well and relax to keep our bodies healthy and to prevent illness. Sometimes you get ill simply because there is a virus or bug going around. If your body is healthy, you should be able to fight the illness and recover quickly. If you find yourself getting sick often, maybe it is because your body is run down as a result of poor nutrition or lack of rest.

# Ailments and symptoms

Below are some common ailments experienced by teenagers and their symptoms. Match up the ailments with the correct symptoms. The first one has been done for you.

**abc** **Ailment**
A complaint or illness.

| Ailment | Symptom |
|---|---|
| | Body aches and pains |
| | Cough and runny nose |
| Flu | Nausea and vomiting |
| | Pale skin and weakness |
| | Tiredness and poor concentration |
| | Diarrhoea |
| Stomach bug (gastroenteritis) | Abdominal cramps |
| | Loss of appetite |
| | Fever |
| | Fainting or feeling faint |
| Iron deficiency (anaemia) | Chills |
| | Fast pulse |

**abc** **Symptom**
A sign or indication of a medical condition. A cough is an example of a symptom.

If you think you have any of these ailments, you should tell your parent or guardian so that you can see a doctor if necessary.

# ■ Visiting the doctor ■

There is no need to visit the doctor or GP every time you have a cold or tummy bug, but if it is something more serious, you should go to the doctor for advice. Ear and throat infections can become serious if left untreated, so if you get either of these regularly, go to the doctor. Don't be embarrassed or afraid to ask the doctor to explain something in simpler terms.

For small problems like dry skin or a tickly cough, you can ask a pharmacist to recommend something instead of going to the doctor. However, if the problem does not improve, then you should go to the doctor.

What would you say if you were ringing up to make a doctor's appointment? How much would it cost? If you needed urgent medical attention, what would you do and where would you go?

In pairs, make a list of other medical professionals that you may have to visit and give an example of why you might need to visit them. One example has been done for you.

| Medical professional | Reason to visit |
|---|---|
| Dermatologist | Acne |
| | |
| | |
| | |
| | |

# ■ Mental health ■

We can all experience mental health problems at times. For example, exam stress could cause mood swings or sleep disturbance. However, persistent feelings of depression or low self-worth can be a sign of mental illness such as depression, which should be treated by a doctor. Mental illness is the same as physical illness in that it needs to be treated by a professional and it is nothing to be ashamed of.

In First Year you learned about ways to maintain good mental health, such as balancing schoolwork and leisure, practising mindful colouring and belly breathing exercises, recognising signs of stress, following a stress management plan and thinking positive thoughts. There is a checklist on the next page to see how you are getting on with these positive practices to maintain good mental health.

1. Tick the things that you do to help maintain good mental health.

   I talk to someone when I have a problem. ✓
   I exercise regularly. ✓
   I don't use drugs. ✓
   I don't drink alcohol. ✓
   I eat a healthy diet. ✓
   I try to think positively. ✓
   I recognise when I am stressed. ✓
   I deal with stress well. ✓
   I balance schoolwork and leisure. ✓
   I take time to relax. ✓

2. Identify two areas from the above list that you can focus on for the coming year to help improve or maintain your mental health.

   _____

   _____

3. Can you remember some of the websites or organisations that were recommended to you last year to find out more about mental health and where to find help? Write them below.

   _____

   _____

## Heart disease

Heart disease can be hereditary, but it can also be caused by lifestyle factors such as stress, lack of exercise and poor dietary choices. It occurs when the arteries (blood vessels) become blocked with cholesterol. Cholesterol is a wax-like substance that comes from fatty foods. It lines the insides of the arteries and prevents the blood from flowing freely, which can cause high blood pressure. The cholesterol may eventually block the artery completely and cause a heart attack, which may be fatal.

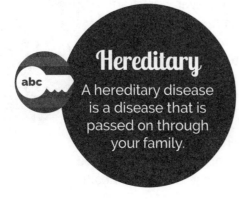

**Hereditary**
abc
A hereditary disease is a disease that is passed on through your family.

**Fatal**
abc
A fatal disease is a disease that could cause death.

Look at the foods below and decide if they are high or low in cholesterol. If the food is high in cholesterol, draw a sad face in the box, as eating too much of these foods can lead to an unhealthy heart. If the food is low in cholesterol, draw a smiley face beside it, as eating these foods can lead to a healthy heart.

**Science, Home Economics, PE**

Steak

Chips

Grilled chicken breast, skin removed

Oven-baked fish

Crisps

Butter

Olive oil

Chocolate cupcakes

Broccoli

Homemade oven-baked potato wedges

Donuts

Sausages

Deep-fried breaded chicken

Fruit salad

List three low-cholesterol foods that you will try to include more often in your diet.

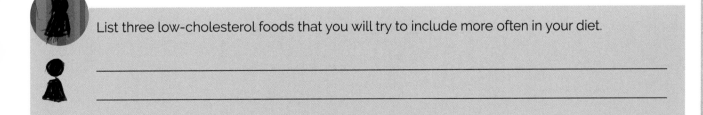

# Cancer

Cancer is a disorder that can occur inside any cell in the body. It is a mistake in the genetic code of the cell's DNA, which causes the cell to grow without control. Sometimes the cancer cells group together and produce a lump called a tumour.

Like heart disease, some types of cancer can be caused by lack of exercise and poor dietary choices. Sometimes cancer can be fatal, but many types of cancer can be cured, especially if found early. You can help reduce your risk of cancer, especially bowel cancer, by eating a diet that is low in fat and high in fibre.

Look at the following foods and decide if they are high or low in fibre. Draw a sad face or smiley face in the box, like you did in the activity on page 33.

White bread

Oranges

White rice

Brown rice

Orange juice

Cornflakes

Brown bread

Pears

Carrots

Beans

List three high-fibre foods that you will try to include more often in your diet.

_____

Tick the things that you do to help reduce your risk of cancer.

I don't smoke.

I don't drink alcohol.

I eat a high-fibre diet.

I stay safe in the sun by covering up and wearing sunscreen.

I check for lumps regularly.

I exercise regularly.

I maintain a healthy weight.

Write a positive message to a teenager who has developed very poor eating habits and is now concerned about getting heart disease or cancer because they think it is too late to change.

_____

_____

_____

## Rapid recap

**3**

Topics we discussed today:

1. _____

2. _____

3. _____

**2**

People or places I could find out more information on this lesson from:

1. _____

2. _____

**1**

Something in today's lesson that I would like to learn more about:

1. _____

**Parent's/guardian's signature** _____

(Your teacher will tell you if this should be signed each week.)

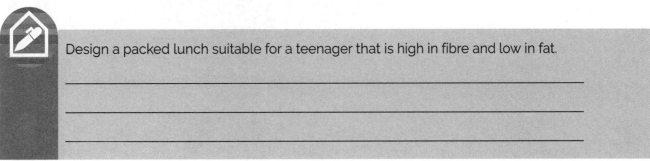

Design a packed lunch suitable for a teenager that is high in fibre and low in fat.

_____

_____

_____

Complete your personal learning journal at home.

# 6. Decision-making

## At the end of this lesson, you will:

 Have developed your decision-making skills

 Be aware of the need to think about the consequences of decisions you make

 Reflect on how you influence and are influenced by others

Key words abc

**Consequence**

**Influence**

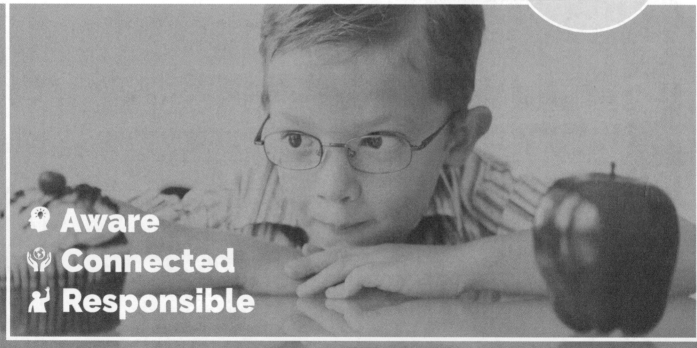

🧠 **Aware**
🤲 **Connected**
👤 **Responsible**

Your teacher will call out a word. Each person in your group must write down three words that you associate with that word. Your aim is to write down at least one word that all the members of your group have also written. At the end of the game, check what the others in your group wrote. If you all have one word that is the same, you get one point. If you all have two words the same, you get two points, and so on. You don't get any points unless *everyone* in the group has written the same word.

# Making decisions

We all make small decisions every day, such as what to wear. In the last lesson you discussed decisions that you make that may affect your health, such as choosing a healthy diet or whether or not to wear sunscreen. At certain stages of our lives we also have to make very important decisions that will affect our future. You are going to discuss these decisions now with a partner.

In pairs, complete this activity.

1. Make a list of the small decisions that you have to make every day, e.g. what to wear.

   _____

   _____

2. Now discuss the bigger, more important decisions that teenagers might make. Discuss who is affected by these decisions and how. Write your answers in your copy. See the example below.

| Decisions I make | Who is affected? How? |
|---|---|
| To smoke or not to smoke | Me (health and money)<br>My family and friends (passive smoking)<br>My boyfriend/girlfriend (has to kiss a smoker) |

Sometimes parents or guardians ask teenagers to make important decisions for themselves or to be involved in making important decisions. However, sometimes parents or guardian make decisions for teenagers without consulting them because they believe they know best. This may cause conflict. Can you think of any examples of this?

# Influences

In Lesson 3 you discussed how you were influenced by other people, such as peers, celebrities, parents and teachers. You also influence other people by the way you act and the things you say and do without realising it.  ⌒ Lesson 3

1. List some of the people you influence, even if it is just in a small way.

   _Saying thank you._

2. Give one example of how you can influence your friends in a positive way.

   _____

3. Give an example of how people may sometimes influence their classmates in a negative way.

   _____

# Consequences

Every decision you make has consequences. Some decisions you make affect other people as well as you. You must consider all the consequences before you make your decision. Read the story about Jenny on the next page. In groups, answer the question at the end.

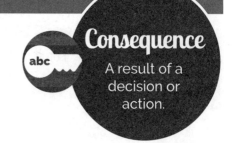

**Consequence**
abc

A result of a decision or action.

# ■ Jenny's story

Jenny has an Irish test tomorrow. She failed her last test and got into big trouble with her parents. Her teacher told her that if she doesn't pass this test, she will have to move to Ordinary Level Irish. Jenny doesn't know what she would like to do after she finishes school, so she doesn't care if she can't do Higher Level Irish in her Leaving Certificate. However, she doesn't want to get grounded again by her parents, as she wants to go out next weekend.

Jenny starts studying, but then she gets a text from Patrick Clarke in Fifth Year, who she really fancies. She replies and they start chatting. After an hour she says that she had better go and study, but he says not to bother – can't she just copy the person beside her? Jenny sits beside Jane Martin and she knows that she is excellent at Irish; it would be easy to copy from her when the teacher isn't looking. After a few minutes, Jenny decides that this is exactly what she will do and she keeps chatting to Patrick for another two hours.

What are the possible consequences, both good and bad, of Jenny's decision?

_____

_____

_____

_____

# The decision-making process

All relationships involve making small and big decisions. Some decisions LAST a lifetime. Below are some factors that you should consider before you make a big decision.

**Look at who is influencing you.** Is someone trying to persuade you? Why are they influencing your decision? Do they have your best interests at heart?

**Are you in a good state of mind?** If you are feeling good about yourself, you are more likely to make good decisions for yourself. If you are not feeling confident or are under the influence of alcohol or drugs, you are more likely to give in to pressure or make poor decisions.

**Set your own standards.** Think about what you are or are not willing to do before you get into tricky situations.

**Think about the consequences.** What are they? How will they affect you and others?

When you are making decisions, give yourself time. If you are not 100% sure, then delay the decision-making. Once you do something you can't undo it, so get all the facts before you make any big decisions. Remember, some decisions LAST a lifetime.

**TOUGH DECISIONS AHEAD**

# Patrick's story

Read Patrick's story below, then as a class use the decision-making process to help Patrick make a decision.

Patrick is out with his friends at a disco. They had a couple of cans in Eric's house earlier. Normally Patrick doesn't drink, but Eric and the lads kept on at him to try it and tonight he did.

He has been going out with Milly for three months. He really likes her, but they had a row earlier today over something silly. He texted her to say sorry, but she hasn't replied. She's not at the disco and he is annoyed with her, as she said she would be there. Tanya, a friend of a friend, wants to be with Patrick and Patrick doesn't know what to do. The lads tell him to go for it – they say Milly won't even find out. He promised Milly he would never cheat on her because his last girlfriend cheated on him and he knows how it feels.

You must help Patrick make a decision.

1. **L**ook at who is influencing you.

   Who is influencing Patrick? Do they have his best interests at heart?

   _____

   _____

   _____

2. **A**re you in a good state of mind?

   Is Patrick in a good state of mind for decision-making? What is affecting his ability to make a decision?

   _____

   _____

   _____

3. **S**et your own standards.

   What standards had Patrick set for himself?

   _____

   _____

   _____

4. **T**hink about the consequences.

   What are the possible consequences of Patrick's decision? Who will be affected?

   _____

   _____

   _____

Write a positive message to a teenager who always seems to make the wrong decisions when it comes to relationships and ends up getting hurt or upsetting someone else.

_____

_____

_____

# Rapid recap

**3**

Topics we discussed today:

1. _____

2. _____

3. _____

**2**

People or places I could find out more information on this lesson from:

1. _____

2. _____

**1**

Something in today's lesson that I would like to learn more about:

1. _____

**Parent's/guardian's signature** _____

(Your teacher will tell you if this should be signed each week.)

Think about a time that you made a bad decision and write about it in your personal learning journal.

1. Who influenced your decision?

2. Who was affected by your decision?

3. What were the consequences of your decision?

4. Would you change anything if you could make this decision again?

You don't have to share your answers.

Complete your personal learning journal at home.

# 7. Communication online

**At the end of this lesson, you will:**

 Know how to communicate digitally in a respectful, safe and responsible manner

Understand the consequences of sharing personal information online

 Key word
abc

Sexting

 Aware
 Connected
 Responsible

**Below is a social networking page. In groups of four, see how much information you can gather about Tatiana from looking at her page.**

Friends (363)

**Comments:**

 Lisa Clarke

 Karl Krycek

 Emma Dunphy

 Shane Mangan

 Mark Johnston

# Tatiana Krycek

Single

From Dublin, Ireland

Born on 17/02/2005

**Recent activity**

Tatiana Krycek is at Lilly's Coffee House with Emma Dunwoody and 2 others

5 mins ago

 **Tatiana Krycek**

Hey Em, just leaving house now will be there in 5 xx

13 mins ago

 **Tatiana Krycek**

No more school for 2 days. Yaaaaay! J

Yesterday

 **Louise Dennis**

Tatiana what time will the fun begin tonight???

Yesterday

 **Darren Smith**

Cheers Tatiana. Will def be there, never 1 to miss a free gaf! Will bring supplies!!!

**Hip Hop Killester**

Extra practice for finals on Saturday at 3, everyone must attend. Only 2 more weeks to D-Day!

👍 Tatiana Krycek **and** 25 others **like this**

**1.** What information can you find out about Tatiana just from looking at this one page?

_____

_____

**2.** What could the wrong type of person do with this information?

_____

_____

# What is digital communication?

Billions of people now communicate digitally through texting, social networking sites, chat rooms, email and instant messaging. While this can be a great form of communication, it is important to keep yourself safe while doing so. Often people can be careless with the information that they post online for everyone to see. For example, if a stranger on the street came up and asked you for your name, address and date of birth, you would not just give it to them. However, a stranger can often easily find out this information about you online, as you saw in the previous exercise.

# Responsible digital communication

* Don't use chat rooms that aren't fully moderated or supervised.

* Never arrange to meet someone you've only met online in person, especially on your own.

* Don't give any indication of your age or sex in a personal email or in a chat room. Use a nickname that doesn't give anything away.

* Choose a username or nickname for chat rooms carefully – don't go looking for trouble. Names such as sexykitten15 or up4itboy14 are naturally going to draw attention from the wrong type of people.

* Think about who you give your number to. You don't know where it might end up.

* Once a picture is posted online, it can be copied, changed and distributed without your knowledge or permission. Only upload and exchange photos that you would be happy for your family or teachers to see.

* Adjust the settings so that only your real-life friends can access your social networking page.

* Hackers can access the webcam on your computer, so cover it with a piece of tape when it is not being used.

Does anyone in the class know any more guidelines for safe digital communication that you can add to the list?

# Respectful digital communication

* If you are taking photos or videos of your friends and want to put them online, always check with them first.

* Try to talk quietly on mobiles in public places and keep your music quiet.

* Turn your phone off in places such as the cinema or church or while in classes.

* Agree with your parents when it is acceptable to use your phone, computer or tablet.

In pairs, look at and discuss the pictures below, then write some more guidelines for respectful digital communication in your copy.

In groups of four, discuss the following and then report back to the class. Don't use any names.

1. Are there any rules in your house about when or where you can use your phone or computer?

2. Have you ever been annoyed by someone being on their phone or computer?

# Sexting

* Sexting involving people under 17 is illegal under the Child Trafficking and Pornography Act 1998 (if someone under 17 creates, shares or even just receives a sexually explicit image).

* Any image that shows a child engaged in sexual activity or that focuses on their genitals is sexually explicit and illegal. It is less clear whether provocative content (e.g. a topless photo) is illegal – only a court can decide if a topless picture could be considered illegal.

* Creating or sharing explicit images of young people can result in harsh punishments. Penalties include jail time and a fine. Offenders are also automatically added to the sex offenders register for at least two and a half years.

* Sharing someone's nude selfies without consent or permission is illegal, even if the people involved are adults. Under data protection law, your personal info, including your image, cannot be published without your consent.

**Sexting** is sharing sexual texts, videos or photographic content (nude photos) using phones, apps, social networks and other technologies.

Go to the Webwise website to find out more about sexting and related topics. You will also learn more about this next year.

## Assessment idea

Write a list of rules or advice you could give to Sixth Class
students about sharing images online. Present them in a digital
format that could be shown to your local Sixth Class pupils.

June shared a topless picture of herself with a friend. The 'friend' shared it on Snapchat
and now hundreds of people in her school have seen it. She is too embarrassed to go to
school and too embarrassed to tell her parents why. What could you say to June to help
support her through this difficult time?

_____

_____

_____

## Rapid recap

**3**

Topics we discussed today:

1. _____

2. _____

3. _____

**2**

People or places I could find out more information on this lesson from:

1. _____

2. _____

**1**

Something in today's lesson that I would like to learn more about:

1. _____

**Parent's/guardian's signature** _____

(Your teacher will tell you if this should be signed each week.)

If you have a social networking space, such as Facebook or Twitter, explore the security settings.

1. Who can see your profile/information?

   _____

2. Can you control whether you want to be tagged in pictures?

   _____

3. Can people find out the following?

   Your full name

   Your date of birth/age

   Your address

   Your school

   Activities that you do regularly

   Where you are at a certain time

4. How can you report or block a person?

   _____

5. Would you be happy for the following people to see your social networking page?

   Your teacher

   Your parents/guardians

   Your employer

Complete your personal learning journal at home.

# Strand review

## In this strand, you learned about:

- I am me
- Looking after yourself
- Setting goals
- Being focused
- Staying well
- Decision-making
- Communication online

Look back over the lessons that you completed. In the table below, tick the skills that you think you learned or used.

### Managing myself

- I know myself better. ◯
- I made decisions. ◯
- I set goals. ◯
- I achieved goals. ◯
- I thought about what I learned. ◯
- I used technology to learn. ◯

### Staying well

- I am healthy and active. ◯
- I am social. ◯
- I feel safe. ◯
- I am spiritual. ◯
- I feel confident. ◯
- I feel positive about what I learned. ◯

### Communicating

- I used language. ◯
- I used numbers. ◯
- I listened to my classmates. ◯
- I expressed myself. ◯
- I performed/ presented. ◯
- I had a discussion/ debate. ◯
- I used technology to communicate. ◯

### Being literate

- I understand some new words. ◯
- I enjoyed words and language. ◯
- I wrote for different reasons. ◯
- I expressed my ideas clearly. ◯
- I developed my spoken language. ◯
- I read and wrote in different ways. ◯

### Being creative

- I used my imagination. ◯
- I thought about things from a different point of view. ◯
- I put ideas into action. ◯
- I learned in a creative way. ◯
- I was creative with digital technology. ◯

### Working with others

- I developed relationships. ◯
- I dealt with conflict. ◯
- I co-operated. ◯
- I respected difference. ◯
- I helped make the world a better place. ◯
- I learned with others. ◯
- I worked with others using digital technology. ◯

### Managing information and thinking

- I was curious. ◯
- I gathered and analysed information. ◯
- I thought creatively. ◯
- I thought about what I learned. ◯
- I used digital technology to access, manage and share information. ◯

### Being numerate

- I expressed ideas mathematically. ◯
- I estimated, predicted and calculated. ◯
- I was interested in problem-solving. ◯
- I saw patterns and trends. ◯
- I gathered and presented data. ◯
- I used digital technology to review and understand numbers. ◯

Now write two skills from the list that you think you should focus on more in the future.

_____

_____

# Minding myself and others

This strand provides opportunities for students to reflect on how they can best take care of themselves and others.

## Strand learning outcomes

- Describe what promotes a sense of belonging in school, at home and in the wider community and your own role in creating an inclusive environment

- Demonstrate the personal and social skills to address pressure to smoke, to drink alcohol and/or to use other substances

- Reflect on the personal, social and legal consequences of your own or others' drug use

- Critique information and supports available for young people in relation to substance use

- Use the skills of active listening and responding appropriately in a variety of contexts

- Use good communication skills to respond to criticism and conflict

- Describe appropriate responses to incidents of bullying

- Appraise the roles of participants and bystanders in incidents of bullying

# 8. Expressing myself

## At the end of this lesson, you will:

 Have developed and practised your communication skills

 Understand how you express yourself verbally and non-verbally

 Be more aware of the need to be sensitive to the opinions of others

 Have practised skills to address pressure to smoke, to drink alcohol and/or to use other substances

Key words
abc

Communicate
Assertive
Passive
Aggressive

**Aware**
**Respected**
**Resilient**

# Communication styles

You may remember from last year that there are three main communication styles: passive, aggressive and assertive. Look at the pictures below to help refresh your memory, then answer the following questions.

Your teacher will call out a list of words. You have a few seconds to write down the first word that comes to mind when you hear each one. Then your teacher will start telling a story. Each student will take turns to add on one or two lines to it. When it is your turn to add the lines, you must use two of the words that you wrote down.

**Passive**     **Assertive**     **Aggressive**

1. Describe in your own words what is meant by *passive communication*.

   I Think it could be worried

2. Describe in your own words how to communicate assertively.

   I Think it means Happy and possitive

3. Describe what you think is aggressive body language.

   I Think it means angry and abbusing.

# Respecting the opinions of others

You may not always agree with other people's opinions, but you should still be sensitive to their views. You can show respect by listening to them and asking questions about things that you don't understand or that you disagree with. Use phrases such as 'I feel', 'I think' or 'in my opinion'. You don't always have to be right, so if you disagree with someone, you can agree to disagree – you don't need to argue about it.

1.  In pairs, list some opinions that parents and teenagers often disagree on.

    School     Socialing.
    dinner     what shdddo
    Clothing.     friend group.

2.  List some common opinions that teenagers have that their friends may disagree with.

    shopping
    where to seat in a car
    A photo they took.

# Listening

You must be a good listener to be a good communicator. If someone is sharing their opinion with you, they can tell if you are not listening. This is rude and disrespectful, so they will probably stop sharing their thoughts and opinions with you in the future.

Discuss the following as a class.

1. How can you tell that someone is not listening to you?

2. How does it make you feel when someone does not listen to you (for example, a parent, a teacher or a friend)?

3. What kind of jobs or careers would listening skills be very important for?

4. List some characteristics of a good listener.

*My mom*

*My brother (Ali )*

# 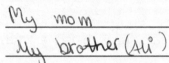 Saying 'no'

Teenagers often find it difficult to say 'no' to their peers or are easily persuaded to change their minds when they try to say 'no'. It is not just what you say, it is also the way you say it. You must use eye contact, the correct tone of voice and the right body language to help get the message across if you want to say 'no'.

In pairs, make a list of situations where a teenager may find it difficult to say 'no'.

Below is a list of various ways to say 'no'. Each person in the group must take a turn to read or act out a statement from the list. They may choose to do it in an assertive, aggressive or passive manner. The rest of the group must guess which communication style they are trying to use. Pay close attention to their eye contact, body language and tone of voice.

- I tried it and I didn't like it.
- I'm not interested.
- Let me repeat myself: no.
- No, I don't think that's a good idea.
- The answer is no.
- I don't think I could do it.
- No.
- No, thank you.

- I decided that I don't want to go.
- No. I don't want to go.
- I don't want to.
- I'm just not ready for that.
- I'm not going to change my mind about this.
- I don't like the way you are talking to me.
- No way.

Imagine that you are writing a script for a school play that aims to teach others about assertive communication. In pairs, finish the script by making Carl say 'no' assertively. Describe his body language, tone of voice and eye contact as well as writing the words that he will say.

**Scene:** *It is the night of the Halloween disco and everyone has been looking forward to it. Carl meets up with his friends in Jack's house before the disco. Jack's parents are away and his cousin has managed to get him a bottle of vodka. The lads have had a good bit to drink by the time Carl gets there.*

**Jack:** (*Laughing*) Hey Carl, you better drink quick to catch up with us! Here, have a shot.

**Carl:** No, I'm grand, thanks. (*Carl looks at the floor*)

**Jack:** (*Walking towards Carl*) I know you're 'grand', but you're sober and boring. Have a shot – it won't hurt. (*The other lads are laughing and looking at Jack*)

**Carl:** I Said no!.! (Call look at him)

**Jack:** You are such a loser! (*Jack shouts in Carl's face*)

**Carl:** Just Stop I don't want to do it. (Stared crying

**Jack:** You are Surge a loser cry baby

**Carl:** I Said no no means no (Carl screamed.

Write a positive message to help Alex, as he is under pressure from his friends to let them copy his homework .

Alex deos want Share his work. he worked so hard and it is going to wards his CBA.

# ⏱ Rapid recap

**3**

Topics we discussed today:

1. _____

2. _____

3. _____

**2**

People or places I could find out more information on this lesson from:

1. _____

2. _____

**1**

Something in today's lesson that I would like to learn more about:

1. _____

**Parent's/guardian's signature** _____

(Your teacher will tell you if this should be signed each week.)

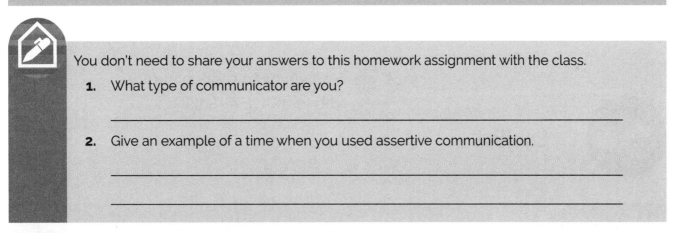

You don't need to share your answers to this homework assignment with the class.

1. What type of communicator are you?

   _____

2. Give an example of a time when you used assertive communication.

   _____

   _____

In your personal learning journal, write an example of a time when you wanted to say 'no' but you didn't. Imagine that you could relive that moment again. What would you do or say differently?

# 9. Family ties

## At the end of this lesson, you will:

 Understand how your role and responsibilities in your family change during adolescence

 Have examined the different relationships that exist in your family

 Have discussed different family structures

 key word abc

Conflict

 Know how to reduce and deal with conflict in families

 Connected
 Responsible

Write down two things about your family: one true thing and one false thing, such as 'My great-granddad had 11 toes' or 'My mother is an Irish dancing champion'. Your classmates will have to guess which statement is true and which one is false.

# ■ **What is a family for?** ■

Think about why families are such an important part of every society in the world. Express your thoughts in a brainstorm or mind map in your copy by using colour, words and symbols. You could also write a poem or draw a picture.

1. Can you think of any songs about family?

2. Do you know any sayings about families? Have a look online if you can't think of any.

3. Do you think siblings in families are treated differently because of their gender or place in that family, such as eldest, middle or youngest child?

# Types of families

Not all families consist of two parents and their children. As a class, come up with a list of different types of families. Think about families you know, families on TV and look at the illustration above to give you ideas.

_____

_____

_____

_____

_____

**Home Economics**

In groups of four, write a definition of what your group thinks a family is.

A family is...

_____

_____

# My roles and responsibilities in my family

Every member of a family has responsibilities that relate to his or her role. A **role** means the position occupied in the family, for example brother or mother. **Responsibilities** means the duties attached to one's role, for example a parent should care for the children or a teenager should help their parents with housework.

Examine how your role and responsibilities have changed as you grow older by drawing the table below in your copy and filling it in.

| Question | In Second Class | In Second Year |
|---|---|---|
| Who was/is in your family? | | |
| What were/are your roles (e.g. teenager, child, daughter/son)? | | |
| What were/are your responsibilities (e.g. tidying my room, making the dinner)? | | |

## Conflict
A disagreement or difference between people.

## Avoiding conflict with family

After you read each piece of advice below, ask yourself 'Do I do this?' and tick 'yes' or 'no' in the table.

| | Yes | No |
|---|---|---|
| Tell your parents or guardians how you feel about things and talk to them about little problems before they turn into big problems. *Do I do this?* | | |
| Tell the truth. Parents always seem to find out one way or another if you lie and then you get into even bigger trouble! *Do I do this?* | | |
| Compromise. If you are not allowed to go to a disco or party, try to reach a compromise with your parents. For example, let them collect you instead of getting the bus. It might be a bit embarrassing, but at least it's better than missing out. *Do I do this?* | | |
| Act responsibly and maturely. If your parents say you definitely can't go somewhere, don't cry, scream or try to sneak out. They will respect you more for it and may be a little easier to convince next time after seeing how mature you were. *Do I do this?* | | |

# ■ Tips for resolving conflict in families ■

* **Confront the person about what is bothering you.** They can't read your mind. Vague complaints are hard to work on.

* **Only use words, not fists.** Tell the person directly and honestly how you feel. Violence will not help.

* **No 'hitting below the belt'.** Don't attack areas of personal sensitivity, as it only creates an unpleasant atmosphere.

* **Forget the past.** Storing up lots of grievances and hurt feelings over time is not helpful. Try to deal with problems as they arise. Don't bring up old problems.

* **Leave out the accusations.** Accusations will cause others to defend themselves. Instead, talk about how their actions made you feel.

* **Don't generalise.** Avoid words like 'never' or 'always'.

* **Clamming up won't help.** When one person becomes silent and stops responding to the other, frustration and anger can result. Both people must communicate to find a solution.

* **Try to remain calm.** Don't overreact, no matter what the other person says.

 On the whiteboard, brainstorm some issues that cause family conflicts. In groups, discuss how these issues can be reduced or eliminated.

# ■ Where to get help ■

 If you are having problems with your family, Barnardos can help. They have a Teen Help section on their website. It is a guide for teenagers in Ireland looking for advice on their personal problems or issues in life.

**You have a right to be safe with your family. If you ever don't feel safe:**

* Talk to an adult whom you trust.

* Contact Childline for information and support. Freephone helpline: 1800 666 666. Text support: text 'List' to 50101.

 Write a positive message to a Second Year student who is tired of constantly arguing with her younger sister for stealing her clothes and make-up.

_____

_____

_____

_____

_____

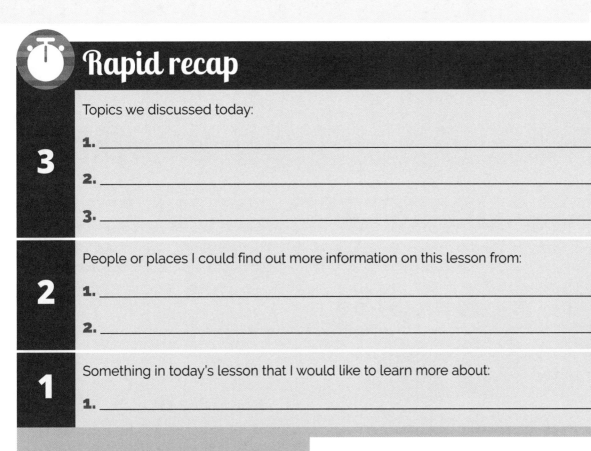

## Rapid recap

**3**

Topics we discussed today:

1. _____

2. _____

3. _____

**2**

People or places I could find out more information on this lesson from:

1. _____

2. _____

**1**

Something in today's lesson that I would like to learn more about:

1. _____

**Parent's/guardian's signature** _____

(Your teacher will tell you if this should be signed each week.)

Think about what kind of family you would like to have when you are an adult. Write about it in your personal learning journal or draw a picture. Use the following questions to help you.

- Would you like to be married or have a partner?
- Would you like to have children, adopt children or foster children?
- If so, how many children would you like?
- What would your roles and responsibilities be in the family?
- Would you be the caregiver, the breadwinner or the manager?
- What kind of rules would you have in your family?

Complete your personal learning journal at home.

# 10. My part in the community

**At the end of this lesson, you will:**

 Understand the importance of community

 Know how to become more involved in your community

Key word abc Community

Connected
Responsible
Active

COMMUNITY

Take turns to complete this sentence: 'When I grow up, I am going to be a ...' Nobody can say the same job twice – each person has to say what the last person said and then add their own job. See who can remember them all, e.g. 'When Mohammad grows up he is going to be doctor, when Josh grows up he is going to be a firefighter, when I grow up I am going to be a nurse.'

# Community

Communities are groups of people who live in the same place and/or share similar beliefs. Your community may be in a certain neighbourhood, city, town, county or country. There are various types of communities, e.g. classroom, school, neighbourhood, religious, cultural, Traveller community, a community based on where you are from, online community, global community, deaf community or GAA community.

**Community**

abc

A community is a large group of people who have something in common.

1. Communities are made up of people, services and organisations. In the table below, give examples of these in your local community.

| People | Services | Organisations |
|--------|----------|---------------|
|        |          |               |
|        |          |               |
|        |          |               |

**Lesson 3**

2. In Lesson 3 you learned about the advantages of being involved in your community. Can you remember these? You also set a goal for becoming more involved in your community. How is that going?

**3.** What communities do you belong to? Why
is each community important to you?

_____

_____

_____

_____

_____

_____

# Community investigation

Go to the following websites
to find out more about how
you can become involved in
your community.

**1.** Log on to the Get Ireland Active website.

List some places in your local area where you can get active.

_____

_____

_____

Read the tips for young adults to get active and write three of them below.

_____

_____

_____

**2.** Search for the name of your local area on Google and find your local area's
community Twitter or Facebook tourism page. Write down three organisations or
groups that are mentioned.

_____

_____

_____

3. Log on to Amnesty International's Ireland website. Find out how young people can get involved in making a difference to human rights in your local and global community.

_____

_____

4. Log on to the Trócaire website. Under the 'Get Involved' tab, select 'Education & Schools'. Watch some of the videos that examine how climate change is affecting communities around the world. Write some examples below.

_____

_____

_____

_____

_____

_____

_____

Write down two ways that you can help to reduce climate change. You may have learned about this in Geography or CSPE. If you don't know, search online.

_____

_____

In your copy, draw or write about a community that you would like to live in. Include the services that you would like to have and need, the people who are important to you and the organisations that you would like to be part of.

## Assessment idea

Read about the Amnesty International Write for Rights campaign (search online for 'Amnesty Ireland Write for Rights'). Watch the video, then research one person whose human rights are being denied and prepare a project on them. Take part in the campaign by writing letters, petitions, emails, tweets, Facebook posts or postcards.

Write a positive message to Jamelia, who has felt very lonely ever since she moved to a new town and school because she does not know anyone.

_____

_____

_____

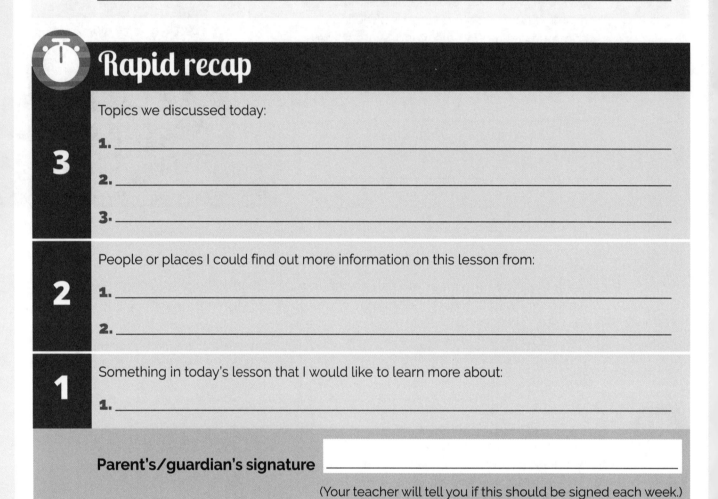

## Rapid recap

**3**

Topics we discussed today:

1. _____

2. _____

3. _____

**2**

People or places I could find out more information on this lesson from:

1. _____

2. _____

**1**

Something in today's lesson that I would like to learn more about:

1. _____

**Parent's/guardian's signature** _____

(Your teacher will tell you if this should be signed each week.)

Find out about an upcoming community event in your area that you could attend, perhaps something that you wouldn't normally go to, like a cricket game or cake sale.

Complete your personal learning journal at home.

# 11. Smoking

**At the end of this lesson, you will:**

 Have examined the reasons why young people start smoking

 Know where to get help to give up smoking

 Have explored how smoking affects society and your health

 Key words abc

*Passive smoking*

No Smoking

Aware

Responsible

# ■ Smoking

Nobody has their first cigarette and thinks, 'Mmm, this is lovely, I think I'll keep smoking for the rest of my life.' Most people actually feel sick when they have their first cigarette because they are putting poison into their body. But they persist until they get used to the taste. Usually they will start off with an odd cigarette or sharing packets with friends. Then they start buying their own and gradually start smoking more and more. When teenagers start smoking, they may think, 'I could give up any time I like – I'm not addicted.' But they keep smoking and they do become addicted.

Put an X on any area of the body that can be affected by smoking.

Lots of people say they are 'social smokers', so let's see just how social smoking is.

∗ Your hair, breath and clothes stink of smoke.

∗ Your teeth and fingers turn yellow.

∗ You get more wrinkles, spots and dry skin.

∗ Every morning you have to cough up phlegm just so you can breathe properly.

∗ A lot of your money is spent on cigarettes, so you don't have money to do things you enjoy.

∗ You get dirty looks from people if you smoke beside them.

∗ You usually have to smoke outside in the rain and cold.

As you can see, the term 'social smoker' doesn't really make much sense.

# ■ Cost of smoking ■

**1,2,3...**

1. In pairs, find out how much a packet of 20 cigarettes costs. €13.50 If a person smokes 20 cigarettes a day, how much would they spend in:
   - A week? _€94.50_
   - A year? _€ ~~8510~~ 4927.50_
   - Sixty years (assuming they start smoking at age 15 and die at 70)? ~~294565~~ 295000
2. What would you do with that money?
   _Buy a house, buy a car, ~~buy~~ give to others_

# What's in a cigarette?

**Tobacco** is made from the dried leaves of a plant called *Nicotiana tabacum*. When the leaves are burned, the smoke produced contains many harmful substances. Tar, nicotine and carbon monoxide are the three most harmful.

**Carbon monoxide** is a poisonous gas. It robs the blood of oxygen, so the organs in the body do not get the oxygen supply that they need. This can lead to heart disease and damage to other organs and blood vessels.

**Tar** is a sticky, dark brown substance. When someone smokes, they inhale tar into their lungs, lining the throat and lung tissues. Inhaling tar causes cancer and lung disease.

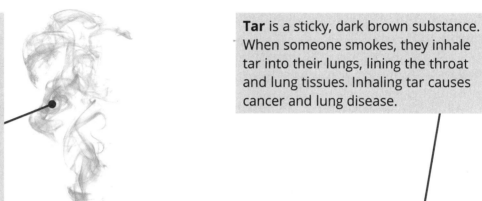

**Nicotine** is a stimulant drug and is very addictive. It narrows blood vessels in the body, which causes blood flow to slow down. This means your heart has to beat faster for your blood to circulate. If the heart constantly has to pump faster than it should, it will eventually tire or wear out.

# Risks of smoking

Seven thousand people die from the effects of tobacco each year in Ireland and thousands of others are ill because of tobacco-related diseases. Smoking can cause the following:

* Cancer

* Heart disease

* Poor circulation

* Bronchitis (the tubes that lead to the lungs become inflamed and lined with mucus)

* Emphysema (disease of the lungs)

* Tiredness

* Decreased fertility

In addition to these, if a pregnant woman smokes, she can damage her unborn child.

## ◼ Passive smoking ◼

Inhaling someone else's cigarette smoke is called passive smoking. This is also very dangerous and can cause health problems similar to those of smokers. For this reason, a ban on smoking in cars where children are present came into effect in Ireland in 2016.

1. Do you know anyone who has or had a smoking-related illness?

2. The number of people who smoke in Ireland has hugely decreased in the last 20 years, particularly among young people. Why do you think this is so?

3. Has anyone in your family successfully quit smoking? If so, how and why did they do it?

## ◼ Effects of smoking on appearance ◼

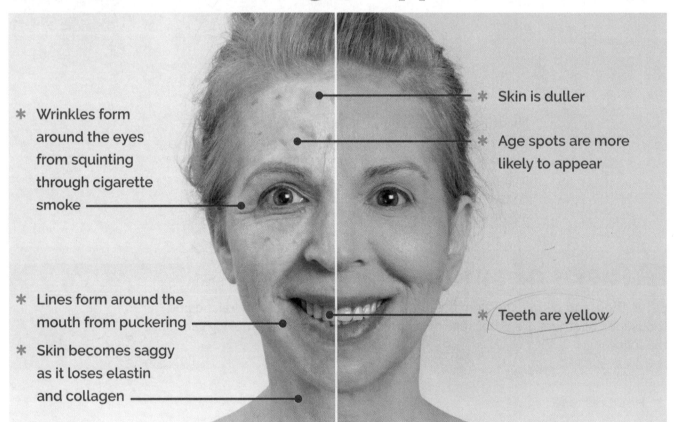

* Wrinkles form around the eyes from squinting through cigarette smoke

* Lines form around the mouth from puckering

* Skin becomes saggy as it loses elastin and collagen

* Skin is duller

* Age spots are more likely to appear

* Teeth are yellow

Go to the Quit website and write down five tips in your copy that you could give someone to help them quit smoking.

HELLO!
FUTURE
HOW was speech
and weekend!?
+ CBA

**11** Smoking

Write a positive message to Joanne, who is upset because her dad has been moody and cranky ever since he gave up smoking two weeks ago.

_____

_____

_____

# Rapid recap

Topics we discussed today:

**3**

1. _Passive smoking_

2. _Cost of smoking_

3. _Whats in a cigerette._

People or places I could find out more information on this lesson from:

**2**

1. _____

2. _____

Something in today's lesson that I would like to learn more about:

**1**

1. _____

**Parent's/guardian's signature** _____

(Your teacher will tell you if this should be signed each week.)

In your personal learning journal, write five reasons why you will never start smoking. If you do smoke, write five reasons why you should quit.

Complete your personal learning journal at home.

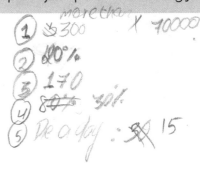

① morethan $300  X 70000

② 00%

③ 170

④ 80% 30%

⑤ Per a day : $ 15

# 12. Alcohol

## At the end of this lesson, you will:

Have explored the reasons why people drink alcohol

Understand how alcohol abuse affects society and people's health

Know where to get help if you or someone you know has an alcohol problem

Key words
abc

**Binge drinking**

💡 **Aware**
🏃 **Responsible**

As a class, do the 'What do you know about alcohol?' activity on FolensOnline, then discuss the answers.

1. Irish adults are among the highest consumers of alcohol in the EU. They drink about 20% more than the average European. We often hear about Irish teenagers drinking too much and young people are criticised for their risky drinking behaviour, but adults often drink irresponsibly too. Do you think that Irish adults drink too much?

2. Give examples of celebrities or people in the public eye who drink or drank irresponsibly.

3. Why do some people choose not to drink alcohol?

# Responsible or safe drinking

Alcohol is a drug that can be used sensibly and responsibly. However, it can also be used irresponsibly. Some adults may choose to drink and some choose not to. It is important to be able to recognise the difference between safe drinking and unsafe drinking. The latter can cause accidents or illness or lead to alcohol abuse or addiction.

In groups, write down some points to describe a safe drinker.

To enjoy alcohol safely, adults should:

▷ DRINK LESS

▷ Know when to stop.

_____

_____

_____

# Binge drinking

Binge drinking is the practice of drinking large amounts of alcohol at one time with the aim of getting drunk.

Log on to the Drinkaware website and look at some of the posters, leaflets and videos that highlight the effects of alcohol. Discuss these resources as a class. Do you think these resources encourage teenagers to abstain from alcohol?

# Facts about alcohol

* Alcohol can destroy brain tissue, which cannot be replaced.

* Between 61,000 and 104,000 children aged under 15 in Ireland are estimated to be living with parents who misuse alcohol.

* Alcohol has a lot of calories but no nutrients.

* According to studies, more Irish girls than boys binge drink.

* Heart disease and liver disease can be caused by alcohol.

* Drinking alcohol while pregnant can damage the unborn baby.

* Alcohol lowers inhibitions, making people more likely to do things they would not normally do. Studies show that teenagers who have set limits on their sexual activity often go further than they intend to when under the influence of alcohol.

* Approximately 120 people are killed each year in alcohol-related car crashes.

In groups of four, complete the table below in your copies. Give three examples. One example has been done for you.

| Why do young people drink? | What can be done to change this? |
| --- | --- |
| Boredom | Take up a hobby like learning guitar, join a club, volunteer, get a part-time job. |

## Where to find help

For more information on alcohol or for advice on where to get help if you or someone you know has a problem with alcohol, check out the following websites.

* Alcohol Action Ireland

* Barnardos

## Alcohol and teenagers

There is no safe amount of alcohol recommended for teenagers, as even moderate amounts could lead to alcohol abuse, promote risky behaviour and damage brain cells. Here are some facts about alcohol and teenagers.

* It is illegal to sell alcohol to a person under 18 years of age, but teenagers are allowed to drink alcohol in their own homes with their parents' or guardians' permission.

* Starting to drink at an early age increases a person's chances of developing problems with alcohol use in later life.

* Studies conducted by the Crisis Pregnancy Agency found that girls who normally set limits on sexual activity go further sexually when they are drunk.

* Ireland has one of the highest rates of drunkenness among school students, according to the European School Survey.

* More girls (44%) than boys (42%) reported heavy drinking (five or more drinks on one occasion) during the previous month.

## Myths about alcohol

* **I can sober up quickly if I have to.** It takes about two hours for the adult body to eliminate the alcohol content of a single drink, depending on your weight. Nothing can speed up this process, not even coffee or cold showers.

* **Beer and cider aren't that strong.** A bottle of beer has the same amount of alcohol as a standard shot of spirits (either straight or in a mixed drink) or a glass of wine, but people often drink spirits more quickly and so get drunk quicker.

* **Having one or two drinks at home is fine.** The latest evidence shows that teenagers who drink at home, even with parental supervision, are just as likely to misuse alcohol outside of the home, and the earlier a teenager tries alcohol, the more likely they are to develop an addiction to it later on.

You know that your 15-year-old friend is going to go drinking on Friday night. What advice would you give him or her about staying safe?

- Drink Less.
- Stick with friends
- who you going with

Lisa is the only one in her group of friends who doesn't drink. She doesn't want to drink but is starting to feel left out of all their plans and stories, so now she is considering drinking just to feel part of the group again. What positive advice would you give to Lisa?

Stop Just leave them.

# Rapid recap

**Topics we discussed today:**

**3**

1. _____

2. _____

3. _____

**People or places I could find out more information on this lesson from:**

**2**

1. _____

2. _____

**Something in today's lesson that I would like to learn more about:**

**1**

1. _____

**Parent's/guardian's signature** _____

(Your teacher will tell you if this should be signed each week.)

1. Take the 'Parent and Child Quiz' on the Drinkaware website with your parent or guardian (on the Drinkaware home page, select the 'Parents' tab, then select 'Parent & Child Quiz').

2. Log on to the Alcohol Action Ireland website. Under the 'Alcohol Facts' tab, click on 'Alcohol, children and young people' and read the information provided. Write down two statistics on young people's alcohol consumption in Ireland.

_____

_____

Complete your personal learning journal at home.

# 13. Drugs

**At the end of this lesson, you will:**

 Understand the health and social implications of drug use

 Have identified health implications of solvent abuse and cannabis use

 Know where to get help if you or someone you know has a drug problem

 Key word
abc

Drug

&#9787; **Aware**
&#127939; **Responsible**

Write some words on this graffiti wall that you associate with drugs.

## About drug abuse

Drug abuse is the misuse of drugs. This means not using them as they are meant to be used, for example to treat pain or illness. Drug abuse can involve legal or illegal drugs.

A person who misuses drugs is a drug abuser. Drug abusers do not abuse drugs – they abuse their bodies with drugs.

Some drugs are more addictive than others and some people are more likely to become addicts than others.

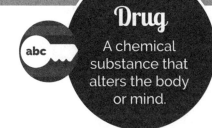

### Drug
A chemical substance that alters the body or mind.

## How do drugs make people feel?

Here are some examples of feelings that can be caused by drugs. There are many more besides the ones listed.

* Fear
* Giddiness
* Happiness
* Relaxation
* Nausea

* Tiredness
* Panic
* Confusion
* Dopiness
* Paranoia

A lot of things influence the way drugs make people feel, especially:

✳ How much of it is taken

✳ Mood before taking the drug

✳ If any other drugs have also been taken (for example, alcohol)

## Teenagers and drug misuse

Most people who misuse drugs start experimenting with drugs when they are teenagers. Teenagers often start by misusing solvents such as glue or aerosols, as they are easy to get. Then they often move on to illegal drugs, such as cannabis.

## Common drugs used by teenagers

| Name | Description | Short-term effects | Long-term effects |
|---|---|---|---|
| **Cannabis, hash, weed** | Cannabis is a type of drug that comes from the cannabis plant, a bushy plant grown in many different parts of the world. It is smoked. | • Feeling sedated, chilled out and happy<br>• Feeling sick<br>• Feeling hungry (the 'munchies')<br>• Pulse rate speeds up and blood pressure goes down<br>• Bloodshot eyes, dry mouth<br>• Tiredness | • May damage lungs<br>• Has been linked with mental health problems<br>• May lead to fertility problems<br>• Affects memory, mood, motivation and ability to learn<br>• May cause anxiety and paranoia<br>• Affects co-ordination and reactions<br>• Smoking hash can cause cancer |
| **Solvents** | Glue, aerosols, gases that are sniffed or inhaled | • Feeling drunk<br>• Breathing and heart rate slow down<br>• Disorientation and loss of co-ordination<br>• Loss of consciousness<br>• Can cause a red rash around the mouth<br>• Nausea, vomiting and blackouts<br>• Airways may swell up, leading to breathing and heart problems<br>• They can kill you the first time or any time you use them | • Risk of brain, liver and kidney damage<br>• Stomach pain, nausea, vomiting<br>• Risk of accidents |

In pairs, make a list of all the drugs you know, both legal and illegal.

_____

_____

_____

_____

_____

_____

_____

Watch the video on FolensOnline about Daryl, who started using drugs when he was 14. Answer the following questions.

1. How did Daryl get into drugs?

_____

_____

2. What problems were caused by Daryl's drug use?

_____

_____

3. What do you think happened next?

_____

_____

# How drug misuse affects the family

The family of a drug abuser is affected in many different ways. Drug use may cause:

* Arguments and upset

* Embarrassment

* Abuse

 Try to think of some more effects to add to the list above.

_____

_____

_____

# How drug misuse affects the community

Drug misuse also affects your community in ways such as the following.

* Drug-related crimes, such as burglaries, muggings and murders

* Increase in unemployment

* Increased dependence on the social welfare system, which causes higher taxes

* Certain areas get a bad name and are dangerous to visit

 In groups of four, come up with a list of reasons why teenagers use drugs. You know the answers better than anyone because you *are* teenagers. One has already been done for you. Present your findings to the class.

● Teenagers are naturally curious and may want to experiment with drugs to see what they are like.

_____

_____

_____

_____

_____

_____

# The law

Passing drugs among friends constitutes a supplying offence. Allowing your house or premises to be used for drug misuse is also illegal. A conviction under the Misuse of Drugs Act can affect future employment prospects and many countries refuse visas to people with drug convictions.

 The Drugs.ie website offers drug and alcohol information and support for teenagers and their parents and gives details of where to find help. Go to the website and search for drug support services in your area. Explain what they do.

 Write a positive message to Orla, whose boyfriend has started smoking weed. She is worried about him and she wants him to stop, but she also doesn't want him to get in trouble.

# ⏱ Rapid recap

**3**

Topics we discussed today:

1. _____

2. _____

3. _____

**2**

People or places I could find out more information on this lesson from:

1. _____

2. _____

**1**

Something in today's lesson that I would like to learn more about:

1. _____

**Parent's/guardian's signature** _____

(Your teacher will tell you if this should be signed each week.)

Answer the following questions in your own words.

1. What is a drug?

   _____

2. Give one example of a legal drug and one example of an illegal drug.

   _____

   _____

3. Think of one way that the government could discourage teenagers from using drugs.

   _____

Complete your personal learning journal at home.

# 14. Bullying and bystanders

**At the end of this lesson, you will:**

Have reviewed different types of bullying

Be aware of strategies and skills to use if you are being bullied

Have reviewed the procedures for dealing with bullying in your school

Know what to do if you witness bullying and know how you can help prevent it

Key word
abc

*Bystander*

- **Respected**
- **Resilient**
- **Connected**

STOP BULLIES

In groups, rearrange the following words to make a sentence. You have exactly 1 minute to see who can make the longest sentence. It must be written down!

buying I when a bus and clothes I like going hate to slow the horse centre giraffe frequently and shopping he tired fashionable that chew flatter run my sit body ice cream have beautifully even I am grumpy large or with my friends or in my car teenage lollipop occasionally on the lipstick

You learned about bullying in First Year SPHE and perhaps in other subjects too. Your group has to now revise one of the topics below. You have 5 minutes to revise the topic, then summarise it in four or five bullet points.

Topics:

- Types of bullying
- How to tell about bullying in our school and who to tell
- Our school's policy on bullying – what happens to the bully?
- Our school's policy on bullying – what happens if I tell?

Go to FolensOnline and watch the 'Fix Me' video that explores bullying and bystanders, then answer the following questions as a class.

1. What type of bullying is portrayed in the video?

   *Verbal + cyber bullying, physical*

2. How do the victims feel?

   *Sad and afraid + ex excluded + embarsed ignored*

**3.** How can you stop this type of bullying?

*Stand up*

## Don't be a bystander

There is no such thing as an innocent bystander when it comes to bullying. Doing nothing when you witness bullying is the same as encouraging the bully, whether you see it happening online or in person.

Bystanders must make a decision: they can either help the bully by doing nothing or help the victim and other future victims by doing something.

**Bystander**
A person who sees bullying happening.

 Why are teenagers afraid of 'telling' or 'ratting'? Why is it easier for a bystander to do nothing?

## Standing up to bullying

Standing up to a bully and telling them to stop takes moral strength and courage. Failing to do so allows the bullying to continue. If you find it too difficult to say 'stop', at least don't join in. If you are afraid of getting hurt yourself, the best thing to do is to get help from an adult who can help. This is not 'ratting' – it is telling in order to be safe.

If you are being physically assaulted, try to get away as quickly as possible and tell an adult who can help. Remember, it is not your fault. Don't put up with bullying. Break the silence and tell someone you trust.

## Where to find help

For advice on what to do if you are being bullied, go to the HSE website, where you will find a booklet designed for teenagers who are being bullied. The booklet is called *Cool School Bullying Project Tips for Teens*.

## Putting a stop to bullying

In groups, go to the Bully 4u website and find out more about how bystanders can put a stop to bullying. Write a few of the tips below.

- Tell someone
- Tell the bully to stop
- Help the person who is being bullied.

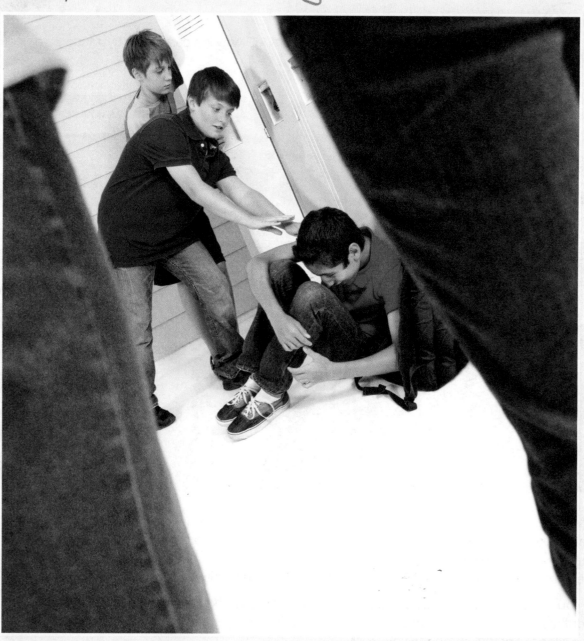

Below are some facts about bullying that will help you decide how you can help to put a stop to bullying.

* Bullies come in all shapes and sizes. Some people who bully may have difficulty coping with schoolwork and may be unpopular with others. Others who bully may seem to be popular, but they are often feared rather than popular. Bullying gives them a sense of power over others.

* Bullies pick on people who they think can't defend themselves.

* People who bully often like an audience. They need people who will cheer on their bullying behaviour to make them feel good.

* Bullies like an easy target. They will bully in a place where they think they can get away with it.

 Write a positive message to a Second Year student who wants to report a bullying incident that she witnessed but is afraid to in case the bully finds out.

_You should be nice + kind to the Person being bullyed. It is best to report it to help the victim._

# Rapid recap

**Topics we discussed today:**

**3**

1. _____

2. _____

3. _____

**People or places I could find out more information on this lesson from:**

**2**

1. _____

2. _____

**Something in today's lesson that I would like to learn more about:**

**1**

1. _____

**Parent's/guardian's signature** _____

(Your teacher will tell you if this should be signed each week.)

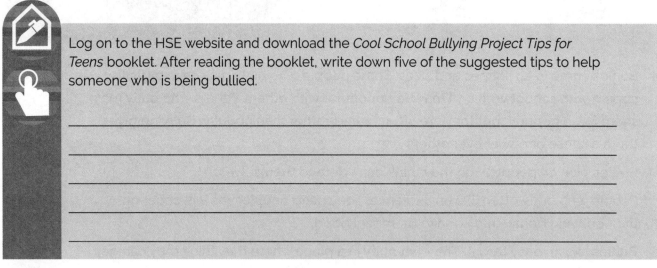

Log on to the HSE website and download the *Cool School Bullying Project Tips for Teens* booklet. After reading the booklet, write down five of the suggested tips to help someone who is being bullied.

_____

_____

_____

_____

_____

Complete your personal learning journal at home.

# 15. Cyberbullying

## At the end of this lesson, you will:

Have examined how cyberbullying can affect someone

Know what to do if you experience cyberbullying and know how you can help prevent it

Key word

abc

Cyber

Respected
Resilient
Connected

Imagine that you have been asked to explain some internet and social media terms to a group of very old teachers. In groups, write down the main points that you would explain to them.

**Cyber**
Relating to the internet or computers.

## Cyberbullying

Cyberbullying can happen on social networking sites, online forums, by email or text. Examples of cyberbullying are:

✳ Mean or abusive messages on a social networking site such as Facebook

✳ Hurtful comments on someone's videos or photos on a social networking site

✳ Spreading rumours online

✳ Posting offensive images of others online

Cyberbullying can happen to anyone who uses the internet or a mobile phone. However, you can help to reduce your risk of being a victim of cyberbullying by following these guidelines.

✳ Keep your passwords to yourself and always log out of a site when you are finished.

✳ Don't post your phone number or personal details online.

✳ Only be friends with your *real* friends on social networking sites and change your privacy settings so that only your friends can see your page.

✳ Be polite to others online.

# ◾ Dealing with cyberbullying ◾

Cyberbullying is never acceptable. If you or someone you know is experiencing cyberbullying, you or they should:

* Tell an adult, such as your parent/guardian or teacher. Tell the Gardaí if the messages are threatening.

* Report the bully to the website or service operator. Use the report button on the site.

* Keep evidence of the bullying behaviour. Save any texts, emails or posts.

* Don't reply to any abusive or threatening messages, as this will just get you into trouble.

* Go offline. Stay away from the internet or your phone for a while.

# ◾ Effects of cyberbullying ◾

All types of bullying cause extreme upset for the victim, but because of how and where cyberbullying occurs – online and at home – it can have more serious effects on a teenager's wellbeing.

* Many teenagers on the receiving end of a barrage of nasty messages suffer drops in school grades, low self-esteem, changes in interests and depressed feelings.

* Bullies can reach others in the one place where they expect to be safe (i.e. at home), which can also lead a victim to feel that the bullying is inescapable.

* Cyberbullying tends to be more extreme. Young people will often say things online that they wouldn't say in person.

* Cyberbullying also allows the message to be much more far-reaching. In just a few clicks, an embarrassing photo or nasty post can be shared all over a website for a whole school to see.

* In the most extreme cases, cyberbullying can contribute to feelings of suicide and self-harm.

Last year you looked at your school's anti-bullying policy and internet safety policy. Read them again and see if you think anything new needs to be added in relation to cyberbullying in particular.

Read the following emails. In groups, reply to them using the advice given on the previous page as a guide.

**To:** agonyaunt@schoolmagazine.ie

Dear Agony Aunt,

My friend keeps posting embarrassing pictures of me on Snapchat. She takes unflattering pictures when I'm not looking, like of me eating or when I fell on the ice. She thinks it's hilarious and so does everyone else. I laughed and pretended it didn't bother me at first, but now it's like she is on a mission to get more embarrassing photos each time. I don't want to be a spoilsport, but it's really upsetting me.

From Sad Sandy

Dear Sad Sandy,

_____

_____

_____

_____

**To:** agonyaunt@schoolmagazine.ie

Dear Agony Aunt,

Some friends in my class thought it would be funny to set up a dating profile for another lad in my class who is really quiet. It was eventually deleted, but then they set up another one. I know this lad would hate all the attention, as he is very shy. I see he isn't in school a lot lately. They think it's a great laugh as he keeps getting loads of messages. I think it's cyberbullying, but I don't want to tell and get them in trouble. What should I do?

From Anxious Anthony

Dear Anxious Anthony,

_____

_____

_____

_____

Write a positive message to Alan, who got a mean message on Facebook and thinks it may be cyberbullying.

_____

_____

_____

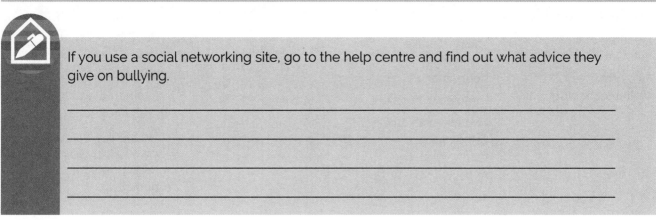

## Rapid recap

**3**

Topics we discussed today:

**1.** _____

**2.** _____

**3.** _____

**2**

People or places I could find out more information on this lesson from:

**1.** _____

**2.** _____

**1**

Something in today's lesson that I would like to learn more about:

**1.** _____

**Parent's/guardian's signature** _____

(Your teacher will tell you if this should be signed each week.)

If you use a social networking site, go to the help centre and find out what advice they give on bullying.

_____

_____

_____

_____

Complete your personal learning journal at home.

## Strand review

### In this strand, you learned about:

- Expressing yourself
- Family ties
- Your part in the community
- Smoking
- Alcohol
- Drugs
- Bullying and bystanders
- Cyberbullying

Look back over the lessons that you completed. In the table below, tick the skills that you think you learned or used.

### Managing myself
- I know myself better. ◯
- I made decisions. ◯
- I set goals. ◯
- I achieved goals. ◯
- I thought about what I learned. ◯
- I used technology to learn. ◯

### Staying well
- I am healthy and active. ◯
- I am social. ◯
- I feel safe. ◯
- I am spiritual. ◯
- I feel confident. ◯
- I feel positive about what I learned. ◯

### Communicating
- I used language. ◯
- I used numbers. ◯
- I listened to my classmates. ◯
- I expressed myself. ◯
- I performed/ presented. ◯
- I had a discussion/ debate. ◯
- I used technology to communicate. ◯

### Being literate
- I understand some new words. ◯
- I enjoyed words and language. ◯
- I wrote for different reasons. ◯
- I expressed my ideas clearly. ◯
- I developed my spoken language. ◯
- I read and wrote in different ways. ◯

### Being creative
- I used my imagination. ◯
- I thought about things from a different point of view. ◯
- I put ideas into action. ◯
- I learned in a creative way. ◯
- I was creative with digital technology. ◯

### Working with others
- I developed relationships. ◯
- I dealt with conflict. ◯
- I co-operated. ◯
- I respected difference. ◯
- I helped make the world a better place. ◯
- I learned with others. ◯
- I worked with others using digital technology. ◯

### Managing information and thinking
- I was curious. ◯
- I gathered and analysed information. ◯
- I thought creatively. ◯
- I thought about what I learned. ◯
- I used digital technology to access, manage and share information. ◯

### Being numerate
- I expressed ideas mathematically. ◯
- I estimated, predicted and calculated. ◯
- I was interested in problem-solving. ◯
- I saw patterns and trends. ◯
- I gathered and presented data. ◯
- I used digital technology to review and understand numbers. ◯

Now write two skills from the list that you think you should focus on more in the future.

_____

_____

# Team up

This strand focuses on students learning about important relationships in their lives and building relationship skills.

## Strand learning outcomes

- Establish what young people value in different relationships and how this changes over time

- Describe fertility, conception, pre-natal development and birth, and the particular health considerations for each

- Demonstrate assertive communication skills in support of responsible, informed decision-making about relationships and sexual health that are age and developmentally appropriate

- Reflect on the personal and social dimensions of sexual orientation and gender identity

- Critically analyse the use of sexual imagery and gender stereotyping in various forms of media

# 16. Gender identity and sexual orientation

## At the end of this lesson, you will:

- Be familiar with terms associated with sexual orientation and gender identity

- Have analysed gender stereotyping in the media

- Have reflected on personal and social dimensions of sexual orientation and gender identity

- Know how to support an LGBT friend

key words
abc

Gender
identity
Homosexual
Heterosexual

- **Aware**
- **Respected**
- **Connected**

# Sex and sexuality

It is important to understand that **sex** and **sexuality** are two different things.

## Sex

Sex refers to whether a person is male or female. Sex is also commonly used as an abbreviation to refer to sexual intercourse.

Your teacher will drum a beat on the desk and the class must copy it. The next person will drum their beat and the class will copy them too. Continue until everyone has had a turn. Make some beats slow and short; others should be faster and more complicated.

## Sexuality

Sexuality is about how you think, act and feel. Your sexuality depends on your body image, gender, identity, gender role and sexual orientation. It includes attitudes, values, knowledge and behaviours.

## Sexual orientation

Part of your sexuality is your sexual orientation. This means whether you fancy boys or girls or if you fancy both. During your teenage years you might feel unsure about your sexuality or who you find attractive. **'Homosexual'** or 'gay' is the term used to describe people who are attracted to people of the same sex. **'Heterosexual'** or 'straight' refers to people who are attracted to the opposite sex. **Bisexual** people are attracted to both sexes.

You don't have to tell your friends anything about your sexuality or who you fancy unless you want to, but it does help to talk.

Whatever a person's sexual orientation is, remember that it is only one part of a person's identity. Nobody should be discriminated against because of their sexuality.

**Gender identity**

describes how a person feels about their own gender. For example, a person's gender identity might mean whether they identify as a man, a woman or something else.

In pairs, match the terms below with their definitions to help you become familiar with words and terms that relate to sexual orientation and gender identity.

|  |  |
| --- | --- |
| Gay | A person who is attracted to both people of their own gender and another gender. Also called *bi* for short. |
| Lesbian | The process of acknowledging one's sexual orientation and/or gender identity to other people. |
| Homosexual | Refers to social roles based on the sex of the person. |
| Bisexual | The type of sexual, romantic and/or physical attraction someone feels toward others. |
| Heterosexual | A person who is attracted to members of the same sex. |
| Transgender | A range of negative attitudes and feelings about homosexuality. |
| Sexual orientation | A woman who is primarily attracted to other women. |
| Gender | A person who is only attracted to members of the opposite sex. Also called *straight*. |
| Homophobia | An umbrella term for all people who do not identify with their assigned gender at birth. This includes transsexuals, cross-dressers and drag queens. |
| Coming out | The term for people who are attracted to members of the same sex. Also called *gay*. |

In groups, discuss some of the ways that people may be discriminated against because of their sexual orientation or gender identity. (Hint: Think about jobs or people prejudging them.)

# Gender stereotyping and the media

Last year you learned about gender stereotyping in Lesson 11. You discussed the various toys that girls and boys are given to play with, how boys and girls are sometimes treated differently by their parents and traits that are considered to be masculine or feminine. You learned that boys and girls are treated differently because of their sex, often unintentionally, and that this contributes to our gender.

*My Life 1, Lesson 11*

The media also contributes to gender stereotyping in many ways, for example through characters in cartoons, TV programmes and movies.

Look at the list of traits and adjectives below. Choose three words that describe the gender stereotype of each of the people mentioned in the table below. Give an example of a TV or movie character that matches that stereotype.

sporty GEEKY **strong** *fashionable*
unemotional *theatrical*
BUTCH **macho**
FUNNY *emotional* *smart* DARK
NASTY
ugly RUDE MOTHERLY
ignorant loving bossy
**flamboyant** CARING
tough
assertive clever *gossipy* BRAVE
glamorous
**kind** WITTY STUPID *depressed*

|  | Straight man | Gay man | Straight woman | Gay woman |
|---|---|---|---|---|
| Three words that describe the gender stereotype |  |  |  |  |
| TV or movie character |  |  |  |  |

# Supporting LGBT people

About 10% of the population are LGBT (lesbian, gay, bisexual or transgender). Studies show that LGBT people are more likely to suffer from mental ill-health, often due to the stress of coming out, homophobic bullying, not feeling like they belong or because they lack support from friends or family.

*Look After Yourself, Look After Your Mental Health: Information for Lesbian, Gay, Bisexual and Transgender People* is a booklet that was developed to support LGBT people. It can be found on the BeLonG To or the Health Promotion websites.

Go to the BeLonG To website and read about how you can support a friend who is LGBT. Write three points below in your own words.

_____

_____

_____

# Francis's story

Read the story below, then answer the questions that follow.

Francis is 15. He has always known that he was different from other boys. Last year he finally admitted to himself that he is definitely gay. He hasn't told anyone yet. He feels so alone because he doesn't know how to tell anyone how he feels. If he tells the lads, they probably won't want to hang around with him anymore – they'll probably think that he fancies them. He is too embarrassed to talk to his parents about this. How would he even say it? He has kissed a few girls, but he never enjoyed it. His friends are starting to slag him about never going out with anyone. Now Francis thinks that he should just ask his friend Michelle out. That way everyone will leave him alone.

1. In what way is Francis influenced by his peers?

_____

_____

2. What do you think Francis should do?

_____

_____

3. How is his mental health being affected?

_____

_____

Write a positive message to Ava, who told her mother yesterday that she was bisexual. Her mother started crying and now Ava feels like she has disappointed her.

_____

_____

_____

## Rapid recap

**3**

Topics we discussed today:

1. _____

2. _____

3. _____

**2**

People or places I could find out more information on this lesson from:

1. _____

2. _____

**1**

Something in today's lesson that I would like to learn more about:

1. _____

**Parent's/guardian's signature** _____

(Your teacher will tell you if this should be signed each week.)

Here are some questions to help you think about your own sexuality. You may like to discuss some of these questions with a friend, parent or guardian. You don't need to write the answers here, but you could write them in your personal learning journal if you wish.

1. The things I like about being male/female are...

2. The things I don't like about being male/female are...

3. Am I respectful of other people's sexuality? Do I act differently towards people who have a different sexual orientation or a different attitude to sex than me?

Complete your personal learning journal at home.

# 17. Forming relationships

## At the end of this lesson, you will:

 Have reflected on the qualities that you value in a romantic partner

 Know the differences between different types of relationships

 Be aware of the emotions associated with relationships

 Key word
abc **Relationship
Desirable**

🤲 **Connected**
🧠 **Aware**

Find out the information in this table from your classmates. You can't use the same person's name twice.

| Find someone who... | Name |
|---|---|
| Has the same number of brothers or sisters as you | |
| Does the same subject combination as you | |
| Has the same favourite subject as you | |
| Has the same first initial for their middle name as you | |
| Hates the same food as you | |
| Was born in the same month as you | |

# Relationships

You have relationships with lots of people, such as your friends, family, parents, teachers and neighbours. When you reach adolescence, you may want to begin a romantic relationship. Your closest relationships may often be with people in your family, but sometimes this is not the case.

**Relationship**

abc

A relationship is a link or a bond that you have with another person.

In the circle below, write the names of the people who you have a relationship with. Use a different colour for each person. Or you could use symbols or pictures if you don't want to write names.

If you have a close relationship with your sister, then she should be near you in the middle of the circle. If you have a friendly relationship with a neighbour but you are not very close, then you should put them near the outside of the circle. This is a personal activity – you don't need to share what you write with the class.

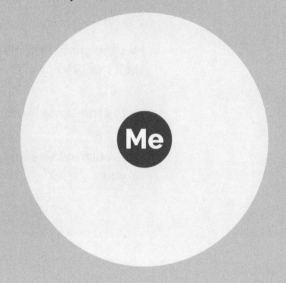

Me

Nobody is perfect – everyone has good and bad qualities. It is important for us to know our good and bad qualities and to be able to recognise these in the boyfriends and girlfriends that we choose.

In groups, make a list of 10 desirable and 10 undesirable qualities that a boyfriend or girlfriend may have.

**Desirable**

abc

Something good or pleasing that you would like to have.

| Desirable qualities | Undesirable qualities |
|---|---|
| 1. | 1. |
| 2. | 2. |
| 3. | 3. |
| 4. | 4. |
| 5. | 5. |
| 6. | 6. |
| 7. | 7. |
| 8. | 8. |
| 9. | 9. |
| 10. | 10. |

Last year you wrote a 'Friend wanted' ad. Now do the same for a boyfriend or girlfriend! In the space below, list some qualities that you would like in a boyfriend or girlfriend, but keep physical descriptions to a minimum. This is just a fun activity – you don't have to share it if you don't want to.

### Wanted

_____

_____

_____

_____

## Áine's story

Watch Áine's story on FolensOnline, then discuss the answers to the questions that follow with your group.

- Why did Áine like Mark?
- How did she feel when he asked her out?
- How did Áine feel before her first date?

You will hear more about Áine and Mark's relationship in some of the lessons later in the book.

## Teenagers and relationships

Some teenagers have no interest in having a boyfriend or girlfriend yet. Others can think of nothing else! Both attitudes are perfectly normal. If you are not in a relationship but all your friends are, it can be lonely, especially if they are out together all the time and leave you out. If you want a boyfriend or girlfriend but don't have one, it can sometimes feel like nobody will ever like you enough to want to go out with you and that you are always going to be on your own. On the other hand, if you don't want a boyfriend or girlfriend just yet, you may be wondering what all the drama and fuss is about.

Discuss the advantages and disadvantages of teenagers being in serious relationships.

Write a positive message to Cían, who feels left out because he is the only one of his friends who isn't seeing someone.

_____

_____

_____

# Rapid recap

**3**

Topics we discussed today:

1. _____

2. _____

3. _____

**2**

People or places I could find out more information on this lesson from:

1. _____

2. _____

**1**

Something in today's lesson that I would like to learn more about:

1. _____

**Parent's/guardian's signature** _____

(Your teacher will tell you if this should be signed each week.)

In your personal learning journal, make a list of five qualities that you have that would make you a good boyfriend or girlfriend. You don't have to show this to anyone.

Complete your personal learning journal at home.

# 18. Managing relationships

**At the end of this lesson, you will:**

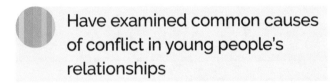 Have examined common causes of conflict in young people's relationships

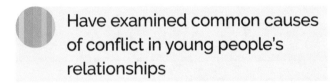 Have practised and developed skills for resolving conflict

key word **abc** Conflict

🧠 **Aware**
🤝 **Respected**
🌱 **Resilient**

What songs do you know about love? What is the message of the song? Write some of the lines from the songs in your copy. Sing them if you can or play some online. Do you think they are realistic messages?

# ■ Conflict in relationships

Contrary to what we see on TV, relationships are not always easy. Successful long-term relationships involve ongoing effort and compromise. There are many things that can cause arguments or conflict in each relationship that we have.

In groups, discuss a TV programme or movie in which there is conflict in a particular relationship (for example, a marriage or relationship ending or someone in the relationship lying to the other person or keeping a secret from them). Answer the following questions in relation to this conflict.

**1.** What is the cause of the conflict?

_____

**2.** What advice would you give to each of the characters?

_____

_____

In pairs, list common causes of conflict in a teenager's relationships with boyfriends/girlfriends or friends/peers.

_____

_____

_____

You have just discussed common causes of conflict in teenage relationships. Now as a class, discuss the ways that teenagers can deal with that conflict. Discuss whether this way to deal with conflict is effective and how it makes the people involved feel.

# Áine's story

Do you remember Áine from the last lesson? What did she tell us? Watch and listen to Áine's story about conflict in her relationship with Mark. In groups, discuss the answers to the questions that follow.

1. What is the source of conflict in Áine and Mark's relationship?

   _____
   _____
   _____
   _____

2. How does Áine feel?

   _____
   _____
   _____
   _____

3. What do you think she should do? (Look back at page 62 in Lesson 9 for tips on how to resolve conflict.)  Lesson 9

   _____
   _____
   _____
   _____

4. Your group must write one of the two role plays below and then act it out for the class. Your teacher will tell you which role play your group will be writing.

   **Role play A**

   Áine confronts Mark about what is upsetting her. She does not follow any of the tips for resolving conflict. They do not resolve the problem – in fact, things just get worse.

   **Role play B**

   Áine talks to Mark about the problems that she sees in their relationship. She follows the tips for resolving conflict. They are both happy at the end of the discussion.

# Mark's story

Now watch and listen to Mark's side of the story. Answer the questions that follow.

**1.** How are Mark's friends/peers pressuring him?

_____

_____

_____

_____

_____

_____

**2.** What might happen if Mark pretends to the lads that he and Áine are having sex?

_____

_____

_____

_____

_____

_____

_____

_____

**3.** What do you think Mark should do?

_____

_____

_____

_____

_____

_____

_____

Write a positive message to Klaudija, who has been going out with Tomás for six months but is tired of the constant arguments they have over silly things.

_____

_____

_____

# Rapid recap

**3**

Topics we discussed today:

1. _____

2. _____

3. _____

**2**

People or places I could find out more information on this lesson from:

1. _____

2. _____

**1**

Something in today's lesson that I would like to learn more about:

1. _____

**Parent's/guardian's signature** _____

(Your teacher will tell you if this should be signed each week.)

Write a list of emotions a young person might feel if they are arguing with a boyfriend/girlfriend or friend and that person stops talking to them. Is this a good way to solve conflict?

_____

_____

_____

Complete your personal learning journal at home.

# 19. Healthy relationships

## At the end of this lesson, you will:

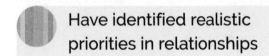 Have identified realistic priorities in relationships

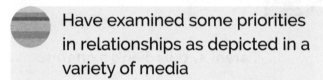 Have examined some priorities in relationships as depicted in a variety of media

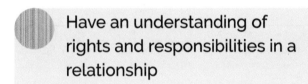 Have an understanding of rights and responsibilities in a relationship

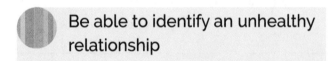 Be able to identify an unhealthy relationship

 Key words

**Rights**
**Responsibilities**
**Sexually transmitted infection (STI)**

🧠 **Aware**
🤲 **Connected**
🏃 **Responsible**

Your teacher will put up Agree and Disagree signs on different sides of the classroom. Stand at the right place in the classroom according to whether you agree or disagree with the following statements.

- If you have a boyfriend or girlfriend, they should be your best friend.
- Men and women want different things.
- You should have the same opinions as your boyfriend or girlfriend.
- Friends should come before boyfriends or girlfriends.
- It's easy to end a relationship.
- Teenagers are too young for serious relationships.
- Marriage should be for life.
- You should have the same hobbies as your boyfriend or girlfriend.

# Priorities in a relationship

Below is a list of priorities that some people may have in their relationships. Read through the list of priorities. If you were to pick a partner for the rest of your life, which of these priorities would be in your top five? Rate them in order from 1 to 5, with 1 being the most important.

1,2,3...

My partner should always look good.

My partner should always support me when I have a problem.

I should be the boss in the relationship.

My partner and I should always be faithful to each other.

My partner should make me laugh.

My partner should be reliable.

My partner should tell the world how he/she feels about me.

*Continued*

I should always feel safe with my partner.

My partner should be rich

My partner should be famous.

I should always receive fantastic gifts for birthdays and anniversaries.

My partner should be a good parent.

I should always be able to trust my partner.

 Read the above list of priorities again. If a TV or movie star was going to be picked for Boyfriend/Girlfriend of the Year by a big media company, what top three priorities do you think the media company would base their choice on? Do they differ from reality?

# Rights in a relationship

**Right**
Something that you are entitled to.

abc

If you choose to be in a relationship, you have a **right** to:

* **Be treated with respect:** Your partner should always treat you as an equal.

* **Not be hurt physically or emotionally:** You should feel safe in the relationship at all times. Abuse is never deserved and is never your fault.

* **Refuse sex or affection at any time:** Even if you have had sex before, you have the right to refuse sex for any reason.

* **Have friends and activities apart from your boyfriend or girlfriend:** Spending time apart, with male or female friends or with family, is normal and healthy.

* **Disagree:** You have the right to think differently and your partner needs to respect your opinions.

* **Not be harassed:** You should not be harassed, threatened or made to feel guilty for ending a relationship or for not wanting to do something your partner wants you to do.

# Responsibilities in a relationship

Along with rights come **responsibilities**. If you are in a relationship, you have certain responsibilities towards your partner.

**Responsibility**
A duty attached to one's role. For example, it is a parent's responsibility to care for their children.

Use the list of rights on the previous page to help you write down some of the responsibilities that you have in a relationship. One example has been done for you.

I have a responsibility to:

1. _Treat my partner with respect._ _____

2. _____

3. _____

4. _____

5. _____

# Pressure in relationships

In a healthy relationship, a partner can ask you to do something but will respect your opinion if you say no. However, in an unhealthy relationship, teenagers may feel under pressure to do things that they don't want to do and may be ridiculed or intimidated if they don't agree to do it, for example sexual activity, drinking or taking drugs.

# Órla's story

Watch Órla's story on FolensOnline about the pressure she is feeling in her relationship. In pairs, discuss the answers to the following questions.

**1.** Why is Órla feeling pressure from Laura?

_____

_____

**2.** Is Laura respecting Órla's rights?

_____

_____

**3.** Is it a healthy relationship?

_____

_____

# Safety in a sexual relationship

The age of consent in Ireland for sexual intercourse is 17. Most teenagers are over 17 when they first have sex. However, some teenagers choose to have a sexual relationship before this age. It is important that they are always aware of their own personal safety relating to any decisions that they make about sex. Along with the risk of an unplanned pregnancy, there is also the risk of catching a sexually transmitted infection (STI). You will learn more about STIs in SPHE next year and in Senior Cycle.

STIs are passed on during sex and are caused by specific bacteria and viruses. In some cases, you may be at risk even if you don't have full sex. Kissing and touching each other's genitals may pass on some STIs. There are over 25 STIs and most of them can be treated, especially if caught early. The most common STIs in Ireland are genital warts, genital herpes and chlamydia.

> **Sexually transmitted infection (STI)**
> An infection that is passed on from an infected partner through sexual activity.

The only sure way to avoid getting an STI is by avoiding any intimate touching with a partner. In an intimate relationship, you can reduce your risk by:

* Using condoms

* Limiting the number of partners you have – the more partners you have, the greater your chance of coming into contact with an infected person

* Talking to your partner about STIs and practising safe sex

To find out more about this topic, go to the B4uDecide website, where you can take quizzes, watch videos and get information about all aspects of relationships.

# Arlene's story

Watch Arlene's story on FolensOnline about the pressures she is feeling in her relationship. In groups, discuss the answers to the following questions.

1. Why does Arlene feel pressurised?

   _____

   _____

   _____

2. Is Gary intentionally pressurising her?

   _____

   _____

   _____

3. Is drinking to 'help her relax' a good idea?

   _____

   _____

   _____

   _____

## Assessment idea

1,2,3...

Prepare some graphs to show the results of surveys on young people's sexual activity, based on reports that have already been written. For example, you could create a graph showing the number of teenage pregnancies in Ireland last year or the age of first sexual intercourse as reported in surveys. You can find recent reports on the B4uDecide and Crisis Pregnancy Programme websites.

Write a positive message to Cáit. She likes her boyfriend, Liam, but feels that he always makes jokes about her in front of others. It's making her feel down, but she doesn't want to say anything in case he thinks she is being too sensitive.

_____

_____

_____

## ⏱ Rapid recap

**3**

Topics we discussed today:

1. _____

2. _____

3. _____

**2**

People or places I could find out more information on this lesson from:

1. _____

2. _____

**1**

Something in today's lesson that I would like to learn more about:

1. _____

**Parent's/guardian's signature** _____

(Your teacher will tell you if this should be signed each week.)

Talk to your parents/guardians about this topic. Ask them for the best piece of relationship advice that they were ever given.

Complete your personal learning journal at home.

# 20. From conception to birth

## At the end of this lesson, you will:

 Have revised your knowledge of the male and female reproductive systems

8/3/22

 Understand the developmental stages from conception to birth

 **Key words**
abc

Conception

Embryo

Foetus

Caesarean section

Awar

Respon

# Looking back

In pairs, revise the male and female reproductive system on pages 111 and 116 of *My Life 1* or watch the video animations on FolensOnline. Label the blank diagrams below.

Everyone in the class should take a turn to name an animal and then what the young of that particular animal is called. For example, the first person could say 'dog, puppy'.

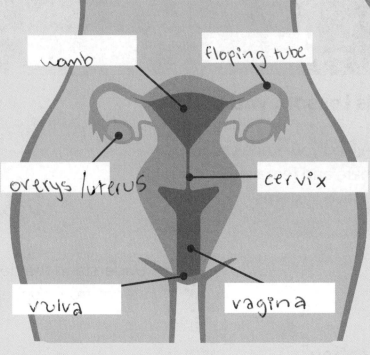

womb

floping tube

overys luterus

cervix

vulva

vagina

*My Life 1,*
**Lesson 19**

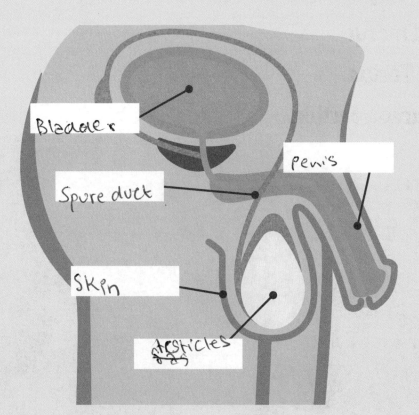

Bladder

penis

Spure duct

Skin

testicles

*My Life 1,*
**Lesson 20**

Team up

# The menstrual cycle

Watch the video on FolensOnline about the menstrual cycle, then working in pairs, make up a question to the answers below. The first one has been done for you.

1. Q. What is released from the ovaries each month?

   A. An egg or ova

2. Q. _egg_

   A. The fallopian tubes

3. Q. _fulling tube_

   A. The womb develops a lining of blood and tissue

4. Q. _womb love     5 days_

   A. Through the cervix and vagina

5. Q. _filerbtion cyele   menstrul cycle_

   A. 28 days

# Conception

In order for a sperm to fertilise an egg, sexual intercourse (sex) must take place. When a man is aroused, he will get an erection. This enables him to put his penis inside the woman's vagina.

During sex, the penis may release small amounts of semen (fluid containing sperm), but most of the semen is released when the man reaches climax. This is called ejaculation. The sperm swim up through the cervix and into the womb.

If there is an egg in the fallopian tubes, the sperm may go through the wall of the egg and join with it. If this happens, fertilisation, or conception, has occurred and a new life has begun. Semen contains millions of sperm, but only one is needed to fertilise the egg. Normally the ovaries only produce one egg every month.

Fertilisation is most likely to happen up to three days after ovulation.

# Pregnancy

## Stage 1 (weeks 1–12)

* Once an egg has been fertilised, it divides several times and forms a ball of cells.

* After about seven days, the fertilised egg travels down the fallopian tube and into the womb.

* The womb develops a lining of blood and tissue.

* The ball of cells then attaches itself to the wall of the womb, which is now lined in preparation for it.

* The ball of cells is now called an embryo.

* Over time, the lining of the womb will develop into a placenta, which will protect and feed the embryo.

* An umbilical cord also begins to form. This attaches the embryo to the placenta.

* Through the placenta and the umbilical cord, the embryo will receive oxygen and nutrients from the mother. For this reason, it is very important that she eats well to make sure the baby gets the correct nutrition.

* By 12 weeks the embryo has taken the shape of a human body. It has eyelids and sex organs and is about 6 cm long.

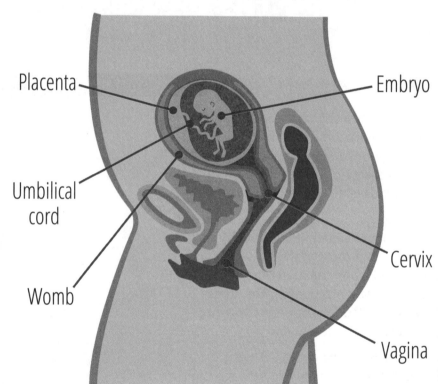

## Stage 2 (weeks 13–28)

* Cells group together to form tissue. The embryo develops into a foetus, forming limbs and organs such as the heart and brain.

* The foetus is surrounded by amniotic fluid contained in a sac in the womb. The amniotic fluid protects the foetus as the mother moves and goes on with her everyday life.

* By 20 weeks, eyebrows, eyelashes, fingernails and toenails have formed.

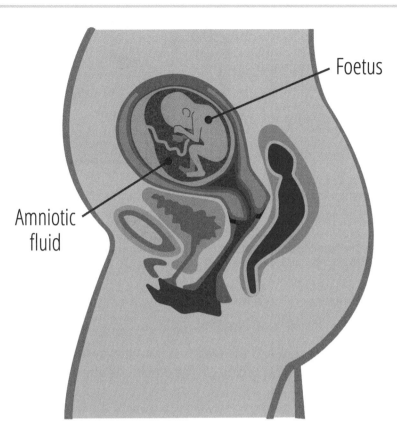

Foetus

Amniotic
fluid

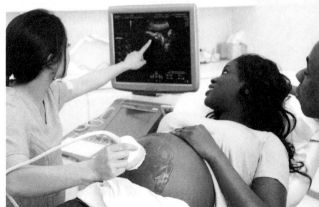

## Stage 3 (weeks 29–40)

* In this final stage of pregnancy, the foetus has developed all of its organs but is not strong enough yet to survive outside of the womb.

* During these three months, the foetus continues to grow and develop.

* By 32 weeks, the eyes can open and close and sense changes in light.

* The baby is considered full term at 37 weeks, but is usually born at around 40 weeks.

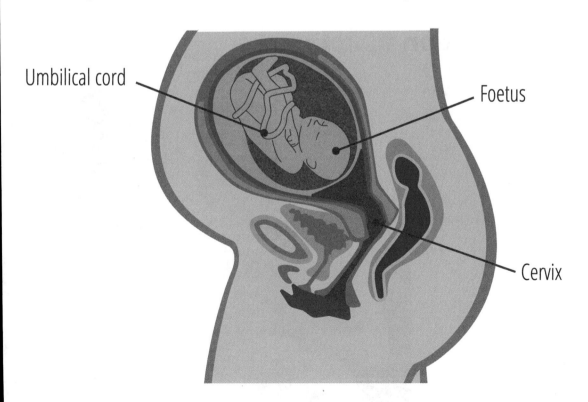

Umbilical cord

Foetus

Cervix

To help you learn about birth, your group must organise the sentences below in the correct order. Number the sentences 1 to 8.

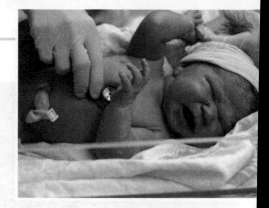

The water sac containing the amniotic fluid may break before or during the contractions and the fluid then seeps out of the vagina. This is known as the waters breaking.

Once the mother has pushed the head out, the doctor or midwife will hold and support the baby's head and help to ease out the body as the mother pushes.

As the contractions become stronger and more frequent, the cervix begins to widen, or dilate, and it becomes more elastic to allow the baby's head to pass through.

After the birth, the rest of the umbilical cord and the placenta come away from the womb and must be delivered out through the vagina. This is called the afterbirth.

The doctor or midwife will check that the baby's airway is clear so that the baby can now begin to breathe on his or her own.

When a baby is ready to be born, the mother will start to feel her womb contracting. These contractions, or labour pains, get stronger and more frequent over time.

By this stage of the pregnancy, the baby will have turned around in the womb so that his or her head is facing the cervix.

The umbilical cord, which connected the baby to the placenta, is clamped or cut. This becomes the baby's belly button.

## Caesarean section

The stages above describe a vaginal birth, but about one-quarter of births in Ireland are by Caesarean section. A Caesarean section, or C-section, is the delivery of the baby through a surgical incision in the mother's abdomen and uterus. An elective C-section is scheduled in advance due to issues with the baby or the mother. In other cases, an emergency C-section may be done in response to a complication.

Write a positive message to Angie, who would like to be able to talk to her mother about periods and pregnancy but doesn't know how to start the conversation.

_____

_____

_____

## Rapid recap

**3**

Topics we discussed today:

1. _____

2. _____

3. _____

**2**

People or places I could find out more information on this lesson from:

1. _____

2. _____

**1**

Something in today's lesson that I would like to learn more about:

1. _____

**Parent's/guardian's signature** _____

(Your teacher will tell you if this should be signed each week.)

Talk to your parents about your own birth. Were there any complications? Was anyone in your family born at home or somewhere other than a hospital?

Complete your personal learning journal at home.

# ■ Strand review

## In this strand, you learned about:

- Gender identity and sexual orientation
- Healthy relationships
- Forming relationships
- From conception to birth
- Managing relationships

Look back over the lessons that you completed. In the table below, tick the skills that you think you learned or used.

### Managing myself
- I know myself better. ◯
- I made decisions. ◯
- I set goals. ◯
- I achieved goals. ◯
- I thought about what I learned. ◯
- I used technology to learn. ◯

### Staying well
- I am healthy and active. ◯
- I am social. ◯
- I feel safe. ◯
- I am spiritual. ◯
- I feel confident. ◯
- I feel positive about what I learned. ◯

### Communicating
- I used language. ◯
- I used numbers. ◯
- I listened to my classmates. ◯
- I expressed myself. ◯
- I performed/presented. ◯
- I had a discussion/debate. ◯
- I used technology to communicate. ◯

### Being literate
- I understand some new words. ◯
- I enjoyed words and language. ◯
- I wrote for different reasons. ◯
- I expressed my ideas clearly. ◯
- I developed my spoken language. ◯
- I read and wrote in different ways. ◯

### Being creative
- I used my imagination. ◯
- I thought about things from a different point of view. ◯
- I put ideas into action. ◯
- I learned in a creative way. ◯
- I was creative with digital technology. ◯

### Working with others
- I developed relationships. ◯
- I dealt with conflict. ◯
- I co-operated. ◯
- I respected difference. ◯
- I helped make the world a better place. ◯
- I learned with others. ◯
- I worked with others using digital technology. ◯

### Managing information and thinking
- I was curious. ◯
- I gathered and analysed information. ◯
- I thought creatively. ◯
- I thought about what I learned. ◯
- I used digital technology to access, manage and share information. ◯

### Being numerate
- I expressed ideas mathematically. ◯
- I estimated, predicted and calculated. ◯
- I was interested in problem-solving. ◯
- I saw patterns and trends. ◯
- I gathered and presented data. ◯
- I used digital technology to review and understand numbers. ◯

Now write two skills from the list that you think you should focus on more in the future.

_____

_____

# My mental health

This strand focuses on building positive mental health, examining young people's experience of mental ill-health and learning how to support themselves and others in challenging times.

## Strand learning outcomes

- Appreciate the importance of talking things over, including recognising the links between thoughts, feelings and behaviour

- Appreciate what it means to live with mental ill-health

- Practise a range of strategies for building resilience

- Use coping skills for managing life's challenges

- Explain the wide range of life events where you might experience loss and bereavement

- Outline the personal, social, emotional and physical responses to loss and bereavement

- Compare how loss and bereavement are portrayed in a variety of contexts and cultures

- Describe how you might care for yourself and be supportive of others in times of loss or bereavement

# 21. Feelings and moods

**At the end of this lesson, you will:**

 Have reflected on the wide range of moods and feelings you experience during adolescence

 Understand the causes of these feelings and moods

 Have further developed skills for expressing your feelings

 Key word **abc**

*Emotion*

 Aware
 Responsible
 Connected

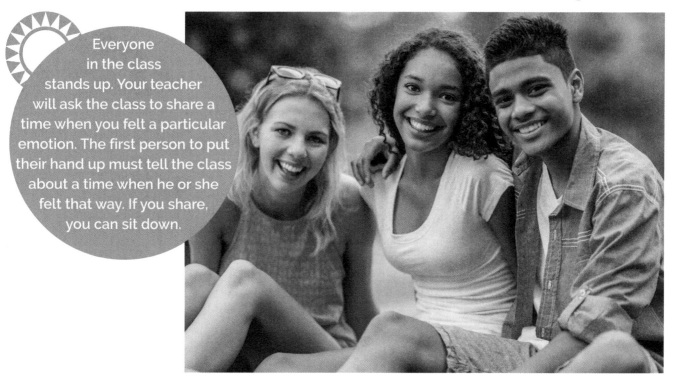

Everyone in the class stands up. Your teacher will ask the class to share a time when you felt a particular emotion. The first person to put their hand up must tell the class about a time when he or she felt that way. If you share, you can sit down.

# Feelings during adolescence

There are three main reasons why teenagers may experience mood swings or may find that their feelings or emotions are difficult to control during puberty.

* **A rapid fluctuation in hormones:** There is evidence to suggest that feelings and moods are affected by a rise in hormones, for example during pregnancy or during puberty. In early puberty, teenagers experience rapid rises in the level of sex hormones being produced, such as progesterone, testosterone and oestrogen. Girls will continue to experience fluctuations in oestrogen and progesterone levels with their periods, which may also affect mood.

**Emotion**

abc

A strong feeling about someone or something.

* **A rapidly changing physical appearance:** This can cause teenagers to become much more self-conscious and worried about image, thus affecting a teenager's mood or behaviour.

* **Stuck in the middle of being a child and an adult:** This can make many teenagers frustrated. Their bodies have started to develop into adults, but often they are not mentally ready to be adults. They can get tired of being treated like children and sometimes get tired of being treated like adults. During this time, teenagers often struggle with identity and are anxious about being accepted by their peers.

# Depression

You already know that being moody from time to time can be a normal part of puberty, but constantly feeling down can be a sign of depression. Depression is a very common condition that affects up to 10% of teenagers. We often think of depression as feeling sad, but depression can also bring feelings of moodiness, boredom, hopelessness, impatience, anger or just not caring. When depression gets in the way of you enjoying life or your relationships or if you ever feel like hurting yourself, that's more than just a bad mood and you need to tell someone.

Depression is a mental illness, and like other illnesses it will not just go away without treatment. You can talk to a school counsellor, a family member, a teacher or your GP if you think you are suffering from depression. You can find out more about the signs and symptoms of depression, how to get help and how it can be treated on the Aware website.

 In pairs, discuss how you may sometimes be annoyed because you are being treated like a child or like an adult.

# Expressing yourself

People express their feelings in many different ways. Some of these are healthy; some are unhealthy.

 Below are some examples of how people express their feelings. In pairs, you must decide whether they are healthy or unhealthy. The first one has been done for you.

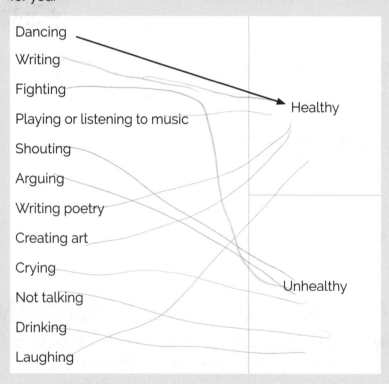

Dancing

Writing

Fighting

Playing or listening to music

Shouting

Arguing

Writing poetry

Creating art

Crying

Not talking

Drinking

Laughing

Healthy

Unhealthy

Below is a list of emotions. Each emotion is the answer to a question that you must write working in groups. One example has been done for you.

1. Question: _How did I feel when I got picked for a part in the school musical?_

   Answer: Happy

2. Question: _How_

   Answer: Flattered     How do I feel when I

3. Question: _I forgot my presentation at home._

   Answer: Embarrassed

4. Question: _How do I feel when my friends leave me out_

   Answer: Lonely

5. Question: _____

   Answer: Confused

6. Question: _____

   Answer: Worried

7. Question: _____

   Answer: Proud

# Dealing with feelings and moods

To help you deal with mood swings and negative feelings during puberty, follow the guidelines below.

* **Exercise and spend time outdoors.** This will help to lift your mood and reduce stress and anxiety. It can be difficult to find the motivation to exercise, so try to build it into your everyday routine. Try walking to school, taking the stairs instead of the lift or going for a walk at lunchtime. Make sure you get the right amount of exercise.

* **Eat a balanced diet.** Follow the food pyramid and choose low-GI foods (see page 46 of *My Life 1* to revise the food pyramid). Sugary foods lead to a sharp drop in blood sugar, which causes energy and mood slumps. The best foods are low-GI foods such as wholegrain cereals, nuts and most fruit and vegetables, especially peas and beans.   ⑤-**Home Economics**

* **Avoid alcohol and drugs.** Alcohol is a depressant and can cause a low mood, especially in people who are prone to depression. Drugs can cause mood swings, paranoia, anxiety and depression.

* **Write about how you feel.** Writing can have therapeutic benefits. Even if you are not good at writing, just write a few sentences at the end of each day, as it can feel like you are getting a load off your mind. You don't need to show anyone what you write.

How would you feel if the following happened? You must write at least two feelings for each one.

- You fainted at the school assembly.

  _____

- Your boyfriend or girlfriend dumped you.

  _____

- Your coach told you that you have to lose weight.

  _____

- Your parent came inside the nightclub to collect you in their pyjamas.

  _____

- You heard that the boys or girls in your class were rating how you look.

  _____

- You can't find any clothes to fit you because you are too tall.

  _____

- You burst out crying on front of all your classmates.

  _____

Write a positive message to Megan, who finds it hard to deal with her teenage brother's emotions. One day he is nice and chatty, but the next day he barely speaks to her.

_____

_____

_____

# Rapid recap

**3**

Topics we discussed today:

1. _____

2. _____

3. _____

**2**

People or places I could find out more information on this lesson from:

1. _____

2. _____

**1**

Something in today's lesson that I would like to learn more about:

1. _____

**Parent's/guardian's signature** _____

(Your teacher will tell you if this should be signed each week.)

Practise writing about how you feel by writing a few lines each night this week in your personal learning journal. You don't have to show anyone what you write. See the examples below.

- Today I felt embarrassed in science class because I couldn't pronounce loads of words.

- I felt happy this morning because my mum made me a fry.

- I felt a bit stressed this evening when I realised that the Junior Cycle exam is only 10 weeks away!

Complete your personal learning journal at home.

# 22. Coping with loss

**At the end of this lesson, you will:**

 Be familiar with the different types of loss you may experience

 Have further developed your skills for dealing with loss

 Be aware of the feelings associated with loss

 Know who to ask for help if you are having problems dealing with loss

 Key words abc

Loss
Separation

🌱 **Resilient**
🤲 **Connected**

# Changes

We all experience changes in our lives. Some changes are small, such as having your own room for the first time or changing your hairstyle. Others are big, like moving house or having your first boyfriend or girlfriend.

 Make a list of some big and small changes that have happened in your life in the last five years. You don't have to share what you write with anyone.

| Small changes | Big changes |
| --- | --- |
|  |  |

Some of the changes we experience in life can cause a sense of loss. As a class, discuss some of the changes that may happen in a teenager's life that can cause a sense of loss. List some of these changes below.

_____

_____

_____

# Family separation

When parents separate or divorce, everyone in the family may experience a sense of loss. It is not easy for parents to decide to separate. Parents don't stop loving their children, but sometimes they stop loving each other the way they once did. Often they just can't get along together anymore despite trying to. This can be a difficult time for parents, but also for the children or teenagers too, who may feel that they are caught between two different sides. The children or teenagers may be confused, angry, upset and unsure about the whole situation and may have many questions.

Barnardos has excellent information and advice on separation on the Teen Help section of its website, which includes definitions of terms associated with separation and divorce as well as advice on how to cope.

Rainbows is a dedicated free service for children and young people. The Rainbows programme supports children and young people affected by loss because of bereavement, separation or divorce. The service is available in local communities throughout Ireland.

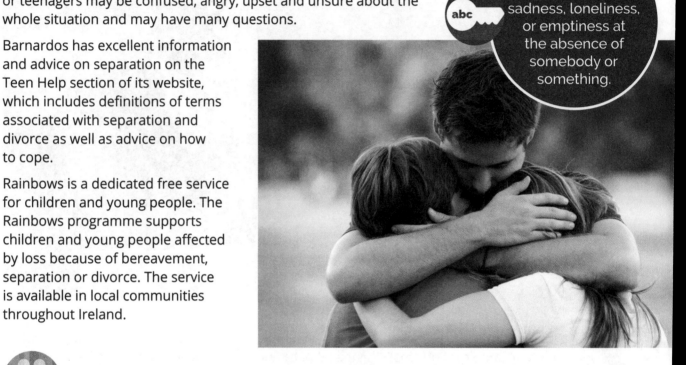

**Loss**
A feeling of sadness, loneliness, or emptiness at the absence of somebody or something.

Go to the Rainbows Ireland website and find out the following information.

1. Where is the Rainbows programme run in your area? (It may also be in your school.)

   _____

2. Find and read the charter for children of separated or divorced parents on the Rainbows website. Discuss what each point means. Write three of the rights below that you think are especially important.

   _____

   _____

   _____

List some of the feelings associated with loss that a teenager whose parents are separating or have separated may feel.

_____

_____

_____

# Coping with separation

It is important to understand that it is not your fault if your parents are separating. Even if you have heard them fighting about you, a marriage does not break up for only one reason. Your parents may not be comfortable talking to you about their break-up, but you have to believe that it is most definitely not your fault.

Having parents who are separated is nothing to be ashamed of or embarrassed by. Consider these suggestions as ways to help you to cope if your parents are separating.

* Talk to someone you trust about how you feel.

* Do the things that you normally do, such as meeting friends or playing sport.

* Take a break from the situation by giving your mind a rest. For example, go to the cinema, play a computer game, read a book or try a relaxation exercise.

* Try to let go of the dream that your parents will get back together. Accept that it is not something that you can control.

* Understand that things won't all get better at once. It will take time, so give yourself time to deal with this massive change.

* You may find it helpful to join a support group such as Rainbows.

 As a class, discuss ways in which you could help or support a friend who is coping with his or her parents' separation.

Imagine that you are the 'agony aunt' in the school magazine and you receive this email.

 **To:** agonyaunt@schoolmagazine.ie

Dear Agony Aunt,

My parents told me that they are getting a legal separation. I'm in shock. I don't even know what a legal separation is!

I didn't know that things between them were so bad. I know that it's partly to do with me. I heard them arguing over the money Mam spent on my new football boots and my birthday present.

I wish I could talk to them. I tried to talk to Mam to ask her about what would happen to me, but she started crying, so I didn't ask anything else. Dad just seems angry. He must be so annoyed with me.

What can I do? Is there something I can do to get them back together?

From Anonymous

In groups, write a reply to the email to try to help this person.

**To:**

Dear Anonymous,

_____

_____

_____

_____

_____

_____

_____

Write a positive message to José, who is mostly fine about his parents' separation but he keeps getting in trouble in school for not having the right stuff, as he can't get the hang of organising his things between the two houses.

_____

_____

_____

# Rapid recap

### 3

Topics we discussed today:

1. _____

2. _____

3. _____

### 2

People or places I could find out more information on this lesson from:

1. _____

2. _____

### 1

Something in today's lesson that I would like to learn more about:

1. _____

**Parent's/guardian's signature** _____

(Your teacher will tell you if this should be signed each week.)

Write down three things you could do to help yourself if or when you experience loss in your life.

_____

_____

_____

Complete your personal learning journal at home.

# 23. Living with mental ill-health

**At the end of this lesson, you will:**

 Be aware of the feelings associated with living with mental ill-health

 Know where to find support if you are having problems dealing with mental ill-health

 Have further developed your understanding of mental ill-health

 Understand that people with mental ill-health can live rich, fulfilling lives

 Key words abc

**Mental ill-health**

**Aware**
**Resilient**
**Respected**
**Responsible**

# What is mental health?

Search online for Stephanie Rainey's song and video '100 Like Me', in which the Cork singer/songwriter addresses mental health. Watch the video and listen to the lyrics. As a class, discuss the message in the video.

Last year you learned about mental health. Our mental health affects how we think, feel and act. It also helps to determine how we manage our emotions, such as dealing with stress, how we relate to others and the choices we make. Positive mental health or being mentally well allows us to enjoy life's pleasures, believe in our own abilities, cope with the normal stresses of life, study well and enjoy socialising and relationships.

However, anyone can experience mental ill-health or be mentally unwell during their lifetime. If you experience mental ill-health, your thinking, mood and behaviour can be affected. Mental ill-health can be temporary or lifelong, but just like a physical illness, mental illness can be treated and managed when a person gets professional help.

Some people develop mental health conditions such as depression, bipolar disorder, eating disorders or schizophrenia. You can find out more about each of these conditions on the St Patrick's Mental Health Services website.

**Mental health** includes our emotional, psychological and social wellbeing.

# Living with mental ill-health

It can be difficult living with mental ill-health or if you are diagnosed with a mental illness such as depression, schizophrenia, bipolar disorder or obsessive-compulsive disorder. It is also difficult when a loved one suffers from mental ill-health. When a person is living with mental illness, it can affect the whole family.

If a parent has a serious mental health condition, they may not be able to work, which can cause financial problems, or they may need to stay in hospital, which can be upsetting for the family.

It is normal to feel embarrassed, confused, angry, worried or guilty if a family member has mental ill-health because it can be difficult to understand and deal with. The feelings may be similar to the feelings of loss. If a sibling or parent has mental ill-health, you may have to take on extra responsibilities at home and may feel frustrated or stressed about this, as it can seem unfair. Feeling guilty about having thoughts you might feel are selfish is also common.

## What to do if you or a family member has mental ill-health

* Try to talk to other family members about how you and they feel about the changes to the family.

* It is important to remember that most people diagnosed with a serious mental illness improve over time.

* People find it hard to talk about mental ill-health and sometimes don't understand it. Try to explain it to your friends clearly. Instead of saying 'My mum isn't well', say 'My mum has bipolar disorder. It means that sometimes she can be very depressed and sometimes she is very elated and excited. It can be hard for us to live with, but she's getting treatment now, which helps.'

* Consider joining a family support group to meet others in a similar situation.

* When you discover a loved one is ill, it can be hard to focus on other things, but it's important to take care of your own needs. Try to eat healthy meals, exercise and get enough sleep. Make time to do things that you enjoy and try not to feel guilty about it. You will be better able to support your loved one if you have good physical and mental health.

## Recovery

Recovering from mental ill-health is a process of healing and transformation that allows the person to live a full and meaningful life. This recovery process is different and unique for everyone. Some things that can aid recovery include access to the right supports, medication, therapy, information and education about mental health.

Go to the following websites that offer support to those living with mental ill-health and fill in the table below. The first example has been done for you.

| | Who can they help? | How can they help? | How can you support them or get involved? |
|---|---|---|---|
| Aware | People with depression and bipolar disorder | Support line Support mail Support groups | Aware charity shops Skydive challenge |
| Grow | | | |
| Pieta House | | | |
| Shine | | | |

When living with mental ill-health, it helps to remember that people with mental illnesses can live rich, fulfilling lives – and so can you. Many famous people have talked openly about living with mental ill-health. Their illness does not define them; it is just part of who they are.

Go online to find out more about the people listed below who are living or have lived with mental ill-health and complete the table on the next page. Do you know about any people whom you could add to the list?

Lady Gaga

Zayn Malik

Demi Lovato

| Name | Famous for/contribution | Mental health condition |
| --- | --- | --- |
| Abraham Lincoln | | Clinical depression |
| Lady Gaga | Singer/songwriter and actress | |
| Emma Stone | Actress | |
| Tom Fletcher | | Depression |
| Robbie Williams | Singer | |
| Catherine Zeta Jones | | Bipolar disorder |
| Frankie Boyle | | Depression |
| Britney Spears | Singer | |
| Charles Darwin | Naturalist and geologist | |
| Zayn Malik | Singer | |
| Demi Lovato | | Bipolar disorder |
| Neil Lennon | | Depression |
| Elton John | | Eating disorder |
| Bressie | Singer, footballer and rugby player | |

## Assessment idea

Find out more about a famous person who lives with a mental health condition and has spoken about it. Prepare a presentation on him or her.

Write a positive message to Peter, who has a brother with a serious mental health condition. Peter loves his brother but is fed up of the sadness and worry that seem to be in his house all the time now and wishes the family could just get back to normal.

_____

_____

_____

## Rapid recap

**3**

Topics we discussed today:

1. _____

2. _____

3. _____

**2**

People or places I could find out more information on this lesson from:

1. _____

2. _____

**1**

Something in today's lesson that I would like to learn more about:

1. _____

**Parent's/guardian's signature** _____

(Your teacher will tell you if this should be signed each week.)

Explain what the following mean in your own words.

Mental ill-health: _____

Mental health: _____

Complete your personal learning journal at home.

# 24. Managing myself

**At the end of this lesson, you will:**

 Be aware of causes of frustration and ways to manage it

 Have contemplated how you may feel in a variety of situations

 Have further developed your skills for dealing with challenges

Key word
abc
**Frustration**

- **Responsible**
- **Aware**
- **Resilient**

Break into groups of four. One person will need a pen and paper. Your teacher will give each group a letter. Your group must write an explanation of an emotion beginning with that letter for an online dictionary aimed specifically at teenagers. For example, if you get the letter A, you could write, 'Angry: Feeling extremely annoyed, a feeling often caused by overly strict parents who won't let you attend important social events.'

# Frustration

Everybody gets frustrated sometimes. People often get frustrated if someone or something prevents them from achieving a goal. Often the closer you get to your goal, the more frustrated you get by being held back. For example, if you spent hours working on something like a school project, jigsaw or painting and your little brother came in and destroyed it by driving his toy tractor over it just as you were about to finish it, you would understandably be very frustrated. Similarly, football fans can become frustrated if their team is playing badly and sometimes that frustration turns to anger and aggressive behaviour.

Teenagers often become frustrated because they are between childhood and adulthood. They may have stress from school and/or parents and they are under pressure to fit in.

**Frustration**

A feeling of disappointment, exasperation or weariness caused by goals not being met or desires being unsatisfied.

1. Make a list of things that make you or someone you know frustrated. (Don't use names.)

   _____

   _____

2. Now list some things that people might do when they are frustrated.

   _____

   _____

# Managing frustration

How we deal with and manage our frustration is very important, as frustration that is not managed well can turn to anger. Anger is not a negative feeling – it is a natural response to a variety of situations. However, some people choose to ignore or bottle up anger, which can be harmful to your wellbeing because the initial problem is never addressed.

You need to manage your anger so that it can become a more positive emotion. Here are some ideas for how to manage anger.

* **Relax:** Breathe deeply from your diaphragm (your belly, not your chest) and slowly repeat a calming word or phrase like 'take it easy' or 'let it go' or just count to 20. Try the belly breathing technique that you learned last year in Lesson 23 or the controlled breathing below. *My Life 1, Lesson 23*

* **Think positively:** Remind yourself that the world is not out to get you. You are just having a bad time. Things will get better.

* **Manage your stress:** Know the signs that you are stressed. Look back at the stress management plan you wrote on page 139 of *My Life 1* in First Year. *My Life 1, Lesson 23*

* **Problem-solve:** Identify the problem that is making you angry and try to solve it. Even if the problem does not have a quick solution, taking one small step to solve it can make you feel better. Try writing down the problem and then write some ways that you could fix it.

* **Communicate:** Sometimes if we are angry we don't think straight and jump to conclusions. Slow down and think carefully about what you want to say and listen to what the other person is saying.

The controlled breathing relaxation technique slows your breathing and heart rate and can help you to feel calmer. Sit up straight with your hands on your lap, palms turned upwards. Relax your shoulders and close your eyes. Breathe in for a count of five seconds, hold it in for a count of five, breathe out for five, then hold it out for five. Repeat five times.

# Dealing with challenges

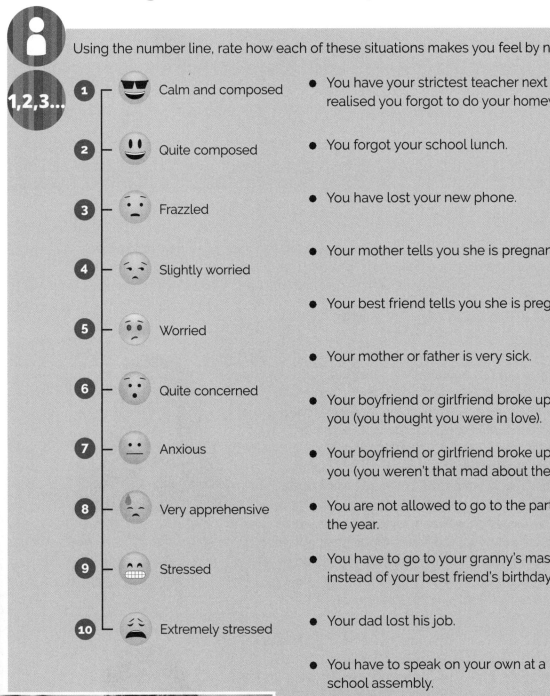

Using the number line, rate how each of these situations makes you feel by number.

1. Calm and composed
2. Quite composed
3. Frazzled
4. Slightly worried
5. Worried
6. Quite concerned
7. Anxious
8. Very apprehensive
9. Stressed
10. Extremely stressed

- You have your strictest teacher next and just realised you forgot to do your homework.

- You forgot your school lunch.

- You have lost your new phone.

- Your mother tells you she is pregnant.

- Your best friend tells you she is pregnant.

- Your mother or father is very sick.

- Your boyfriend or girlfriend broke up with you (you thought you were in love).

- Your boyfriend or girlfriend broke up with you (you weren't that mad about them).

- You are not allowed to go to the party of the year.

- You have to go to your granny's mass instead of your best friend's birthday party.

- Your dad lost his job.

- You have to speak on your own at a school assembly.

- You have to speak on your own to the school principal.

- Your sister leaves home to live in America.

- Your father or mother leaves home to live in America.

- Your parents tell you that you are moving to a new town and a new school.

Last year you learned about coping skills that you can use in difficult situations. Do you remember these? (Revise page 142 of *My Life 1* to refresh your memory.) Choose the most stressful thing you found on the list on the previous page and write three coping skills that you could use to help you deal with it if it happened to you.

My Life 1, Lesson 24

_____

_____

_____

Read the two scenarios below about teenagers facing challenges. Each character is feeling under pressure for different reasons and has decided to talk to a trusted adult. Your group must take on the role of the adult and offer some advice by answering the questions that follow.

Taylor is 15. She has always done really well at school and hopes to get excellent exam results, just like her sister. She is also captain of the basketball team and is very artistic. Her family is very proud of her and encourage her to do well. However, her older brother keeps telling her that she is too uptight and serious. Over the past year, Taylor has lost a lot of weight. She is now underweight and she sometimes suffers dizzy spells. Exams are now two months away and Taylor is getting more and more stressed. She has stopped painting and playing basketball to make more time for study.

Colm is 17. He is an apprentice mechanic and his boss says he is a good worker and fast learner. He lives with his dad, who works two jobs to make ends meet. On weekends they relax in front of the TV and have a few drinks. Colm's girlfriend is 18 and has just finished school. She is putting pressure on him to move in together, but Colm likes living with his dad and thinks they are too young to live together. He knows she is not happy at home, which makes the decision harder. It's on his mind at work and lately he is finding it hard to concentrate. The thoughts of telling her is really stressing him out. He has been avoiding her calls and is spending a lot of time in the pub with his friends instead.

1. Analysis
   - How is the person feeling?
   - What are they worried about?
   - How is the stress affecting their life?
   - How are they coping at the moment?

2. Take action
   - What coping skills could the person use to help them at the moment?
   - Suggest two actions the person could put in place today to help them with this challenge.
   - What would the consequences be of making these actions?

Write a positive message to Seán, who was so angry with his younger brother, Max, for scratching his brand new PlayStation game that he hit him. Seán got in trouble and his dad won't even listen to why he did it. Now he is so angry with Max that he wants to destroy something belonging to him to get him back.

_____

_____

_____

## Rapid recap

**3** Topics we discussed today:

1. _____
2. _____
3. _____

**2** People or places I could find out more information on this lesson from:

1. _____
2. _____

**1** Something in today's lesson that I would like to learn more about:

1. _____

**Parent's/guardian's signature** _____

(Your teacher will tell you if this should be signed each week.)

Write three things that you could do when you feel frustrated.

_____
_____
_____

Complete your personal learning journal at home.

# ▓ Strand review ▓▓

## In this strand, you learned about:

- Feelings and moods
- Living with mental ill-health
- Coping with loss
- Managing yourself

Look back over the lessons that you completed. In the table below, tick the skills that you think you learned or used.

### Managing myself

- I know myself better. ◯
- I made decisions. ◯
- I set goals. ◯
- I achieved goals. ◯
- I thought about what I learned. ◯
- I used technology to learn. ◯

### Staying well

- I am healthy and active. ◯
- I am social. ◯
- I feel safe. ◯
- I am spiritual. ◯
- I feel confident. ◯
- I feel positive about what I learned. ◯

### Communicating

- I used language. ◯
- I used numbers. ◯
- I listened to my classmates. ◯
- I expressed myself. ◯
- I performed/ presented. ◯
- I had a discussion/ debate. ◯
- I used technology to communicate. ◯

### Being literate

- I understand some new words. ◯
- I enjoyed words and language. ◯
- I wrote for different reasons. ◯
- I expressed my ideas clearly. ◯
- I developed my spoken language. ◯
- I read and wrote in different ways. ◯

### Being creative

- I used my imagination. ◯
- I thought about things from a different point of view. ◯
- I put ideas into action. ◯
- I learned in a creative way. ◯
- I was creative with digital technology. ◯

### Working with others

- I developed relationships. ◯
- I dealt with conflict. ◯
- I co-operated. ◯
- I respected difference. ◯
- I helped make the world a better place. ◯
- I learned with others. ◯
- I worked with others using digital technology. ◯

### Managing information and thinking

- I was curious. ◯
- I gathered and analysed information. ◯
- I thought creatively. ◯
- I thought about what I learned. ◯
- I used digital technology to access, manage and share information. ◯

### Being numerate

- I expressed ideas mathematically. ◯
- I estimated, predicted and calculated. ◯
- I was interested in problem-solving. ◯
- I saw patterns and trends. ◯
- I gathered and presented data. ◯
- I used digital technology to review and understand numbers. ◯

Now write two skills from the list that you think you should focus on more in the future.

_____

_____

# Glossary

## A

**Aggressive communication:** A tendency to attack or be hostile to others.

**Ailment:** A complaint or illness.

**Assertive communication:** Confident and clear in stating your point.

## B

**Binge drinking:** The practice of drinking large amounts of alcohol at one time with the aim of getting drunk.

**Bystander:** A person who sees bullying happening.

## C

**Caesarean section:** A surgical procedure to deliver a baby.

**Communicate:** The way to convey feelings or thoughts to others.

**Community:** A large group of people who have something in common.

**Conception:** The action of conceiving or creating a child.

**Conflict:** A disagreement or difference between people.

**Consequence:** A result of a decision or action.

**Cyber:** Relating to the internet or computers.

## D

**Desirable:** Something good or pleasing that you would like to have.

**Divorce:** A legal ending of a marriage.

**Drug:** A chemical substance that alters the body or mind.

## E

**Embryo:** A fertilised egg from conception to eight weeks.

**Emotion:** A strong feeling about something or someone.

## F

**Fatal:** Causing death.

**Foetus:** The term for an unborn human baby from eight weeks after conception.

**Frustration:** A feeling of disappointment, exasperation or weakness caused by goals not being met or desires being unsatisfied.

## G

**Gender identity:** Describes how a person feels about their own gender.

**Goal:** Something that you aim to achieve.

## H

**Hereditary:** Passed on through your family.

**Heterosexual:** The term for people who are attracted to members of the opposite sex.

**Homosexual:** The term for people who are attracted to members of the same sex.

## I

**Independent:** Capable of thinking and acting without consulting others.

**Influence:** To affect someone's thinking or actions.

## L

**Loss:** A feeling of sadness, loneliness or emptiness at the absence of something or someone.

## M

**Maturity:** The full development of something or someone.

**Mental health:** Includes our emotional, psychological and social wellbeing.

**Motivation:** What drives or inspires you to do something.

## O

**Obstacle:** Something that may prevent you from achieving your goal.

## P

**Passive communication:** Tending to avoid expressing opinions or feelings.

**Passive smoking:** Inhaling someone else's cigarette smoke.

## R

**Relationship:** A link or bond that you have with another person.

**Responsibility:** A duty attached to one's role.

**Right:** Something that you are entitled to.

## S

**Separation:** The act of stopping living together as a couple.

**Sexting:** Sharing sexual texts, videos or photographic content (nude photos) using phones, apps, social networks and other technologies.

**STI:** This stands for sexually transmitted infection, which is an infection that is passed on from an infected partner through sexual activity.

**Symptom:** A sign or indication of a medical condition.